The Origins of Christmas

The Origins of Christmas

JOSEPH F. KELLY

LITURGICAL PRESS
Collegeville, Minnesota

www.litpress.org

Cover design by David Manahan, O.S.B. Mosaic detail of *The Three Kings*, Church of Saint Apollinare Nuovo, Ravenna, Italy.

1   2   3   4   5   6   7   8

Library of Congress Cataloging-in-Publication Data

Kelly, Joseph F. (Joseph Francis), 1945–
    The origins of Christmas / by Joseph F. Kelly.
      p. cm.
    Includes bibliographical references.
    ISBN 0-8146-2984-9 (pbk. : alk. paper)
    1. Christmas—History—To 1500.   2. Fasts and feasts—History of doctrines—Early church, ca. 30–600.   I. Title.

BV45.K44   2004
263'.915'09—dc22

                                2004000902

To my beloved twin granddaughters,

Hannah Laine Wagoner and Jenna Grace Wagoner,

on their first Christmas

CONTENTS

Preface   ix

Introduction   xi

CHAPTER ONE
The Birth of Jesus   1

CHAPTER TWO
Creating the Christmas Story   31

CHAPTER THREE
Creating Christmas Day and the Christmas Season   53

CHAPTER FOUR
Jesus, Mary, the Magi, and an Obscure Asian Bishop   79

CHAPTER FIVE
The Popular Acceptance of Christmas   111

Epilogue   129

Appendix: The Gospel Infancy Narratives   131

Further Reading   143

Preface

This book began as the opening chapters of a larger history of Christmas, but, after reading them over, I thought that they might make a good, brief history of how Christmas began. Mark Twomey and Peter Dwyer of the Liturgical Press agreed with me, and thus this book came into existence. I plan to write the rest of the history of Christmas and hope this book will get the project off to a good start.

I want to thank Mark and Peter for their confidence in my work. I also want to thank Ann Blattner who arranged for the illustrations that add so much to the text. This book was written during a sabbatical from the Department of Religious Studies at John Carroll University. My thanks to my chairperson, Dr. Paul Lauritzen, for recommending me for the sabbatical to the University Committee on Research; to Dr. Mary Beadle, dean of the Graduate School, and chairperson of that committee, as well as the other members of the committee, for recommending me for the sabbatical; to Dr. Nick Baumgartner, dean of the College of Arts and Sciences, who approved the committee's recommendation; and Dr. David LaGuardia, academic vice-president, who granted the sabbatical. My thanks to my graduate assistant, Kristie Varga, who read the text and caught numerous errors. My thanks also to my current graduate assistant, Lisa Wells, who made many stylistic suggestions and who caught many discrepancies; this is a better book because of her.

My sincerest thanks go to my wife Ellen who took time from her own busy schedule to make myriad sacrifices, both large and small, so that I would have the time to write.

This book is dedicated to my identical twin granddaughters, Hannah and Jenna Wagoner, on the occasion of their first Christmas. Nothing conveys the wonder and hope of Christmas like a baby or, in this wonderful instance, two babies.

Joseph F. Kelly
Christmas 2003

Introduction

On a snowy mid-December evening some years ago, I gave a lecture at a branch campus of an Ohio state university. I took a shortcut home on a well-paved but unlighted rural road. Going along in the darkness, I saw some bright lights off to the side of the road. As I got closer, I could make out a farm house with a lighted Christmas tree in the front window and strings of bulbs on door frames and plants. There was nothing special about this display, just everyday lighting. But shining in the complete darkness of that rural road, this was a welcome and warming sight. This farm family had no close neighbors, and so their lights would be seen only by anonymous strangers driving by. What a kind thing that was for them to do, to brighten the evenings of people they did not even know.

To switch locales, many years ago I was working in a run-down area of a large city. Many people in that neighborhood lived in unpleasant, cramped, basement apartments with little natural light. About a week before Christmas, late in the afternoon when it was dark, I was walking by one of those apartments and noticed a small but very colorful artificial wreath in the window. This decoration had certainly come from a bargain store, but, inexpensive as it was, the wreath served to brighten that family's holiday season—and mine. These two examples could be multiplied by all readers, and they would prove conclusively what we all know, that there is indeed a Christmas spirit.

Christmas is unique. It impacts us in ways that other seasons and holidays do not. Many people have grown up with Christmas, mostly with happy memories, occasionally with sad ones, but they all wish to make it a joyous occasion for themselves, their families, and their friends. Along with Easter, Christmas is one of the two most important feasts in Christianity, but it is actually the more widely celebrated because even in many countries that are officially non-religious, like the United States, Christmas has achieved the status of a national holiday. Many people who do not celebrate it religiously still observe it as a secular holiday.

Christmas has become such a part of our lives that we cannot imagine a period when no one knew on what day to celebrate it or when Advent did not exist, or, even more amazingly, when Christmas itself was not celebrated. But this was the situation from the time of Jesus till the sixth century, the era when Christians lived in the Roman Empire, partly in times of persecution, partly when the emperors themselves had become Christian. It was in this period that Christmas originated, took shape, and developed into the feast we know so well.

This brief book will tell that story, and when it is done, we will have seen how the gospel infancy narratives arose and what role they played in Early Christianity. We will have encountered a whole variety of things *not* in the gospels, such as the date of December 25, the three kings, the ox and the donkey at the manger, accounts of the parents of Mary as well as of Joseph's children by his first marriage(!), and then the earliest Christmas art and music.

But before we get to the story of Christmas in early Christianity, we must make an important distinction. The birth of Christ as recounted in the gospels is the *Nativity*, but Christmas is the *feast* of the Nativity. People often speak of the birth of Christ as the first Christmas, but really it was not. No one celebrated a feast in honor of his birth until at least the third century and maybe not until the fourth. So in this book, when we speak of Christmas, we are speaking of the feast, although, since the feast depends upon the event, we will begin with the gospel accounts of the Nativity. [An appendix after the last chapter contains the texts of the Infancy Narratives.]

The story of the origins of Christmas is not well known, but it is fascinating and, in a way, remarkable. It starts when Christmas did not exist, and it finishes when Christmas had become an integral part of Christian life and Western culture.

The Birth of Jesus

Although Christmas has made the Nativity the best known of all Bible stories, only two of the twenty-seven New Testament books tell of Jesus' birth, and those are the gospels of Matthew and Luke. The other New Testament books do not even mention the Nativity. The unavoidable fact is that the earliest Christians were not particularly interested in Jesus' birth. Why not?

No one knows the exact date of Jesus' death (nor, as we shall see, of his birth), but it was most likely around 33 A.D. Jesus himself wrote nothing. The earliest Christian writer was the Apostle Paul, an educated Jew from Asia Minor (modern Turkey) who converted to Christianity about the year 35. He never knew the earthly Jesus. Paul wrote his first epistle or letter about the year 50 to a Christian community in a Greek city called Thessalonica. In this letter, called 1 Thessalonians, Paul warned his readers to be prepared for the imminent end of the world, an idea he repeated in some of his other epistles and which appears in other New Testament books as well.

The notion of an imminent end explains a lot about the early Christians, including their lack of interest in Jesus' birth. They saw little need to produce accounts of him or to write books of almost any kind because the end was near. Even Paul's letters are not formal theological treatises, so familiar from later writers, but letters written in response to immediate needs or to crises in various communities. The basic Christian message dealt not with Jesus' birth but with his death, which the Christians believed had redeemed the world from the sin of Adam and Eve. There were accounts of Jesus' words and deeds circulating orally among the first Christians; Paul's letters prove that he knew something of Jesus' life and career, but they make no mention of his birth.

As our existence proves, the world did not end. Christianity moved out of its Jewish homeland into the larger Roman Empire, spreading to Syria, Asia Minor, Egypt, Cyprus, Greece, Italy, and beyond. The continued existence and geographical spread of the Church demanded more organization and more formulation of beliefs. Oral tradition preserved accounts of Jesus' words and deeds, but about the year 70 a Christian known as Mark created a written account, called a gospel, a word which means "good news" in Greek. Contrary to much later misunderstanding, a gospel is not a biography of Jesus, since the gospels concentrate on Jesus' public career and his death and resurrection, a period of only a few years. Mark's gospel starts off with Jesus as an adult who goes to receive baptism from the charismatic, prophetic reformer John the Baptist, but it says nothing about Jesus' birth.

The gospel became a popular literary genre. Sometime in the 80s two other Christians, Matthew and Luke, also wrote gospels, deriving much of their material from Mark's work as well as other sources. Significantly, they began with accounts of Jesus' birth, which biblical scholars call the Infancy Narratives. What had happened in the life of the early Church to bring about this change? Why had Jesus' birth suddenly become important?

Matthew and Luke do not tell us why they wrote about Jesus' birth, but modern biblical scholars have deciphered the answer. Although it may be natural to think that people simply wanted to know more about Jesus, who had then been dead for a half-century and whose disciples were growing in number, the problem there is that Matthew and Luke tell us nothing about Jesus between his birth and public career thirty years later, except for a brief story Luke tells of the twelve-year-old Jesus. If they wanted to give biographical information about him before his public career, why leave out so much? The answer is, their concern was theological.

The Christians believed that Jesus was the Son of God, not in the way that all Jews believed all women and men to be God's daughters and sons, but in a special, unique way. Yet Mark's gospel portrayed this issue in a problematic way. He speaks of the heavens opening, of the Spirit of God descending in the form of a dove, and of a voice from heaven saying, "You are my beloved Son with whom I am well pleased" (Mark 1:11). While that sounds all right, the problem was that this event occurred immediately after Jesus had been baptized by John the Baptist; in fact, it happened "just as he was coming up out of the water."

Matthew and Luke, like all Christians, believed that Jesus had been God's Son for his whole life, and it disturbed them that Mark's gospel implied, even if unwittingly, that Jesus had been recognized as God's Son only as an adult and only after his baptism by John. Indeed, they may have feared some people might see a causal relationship between the baptism and the recognition. So the two evangelists, as gospel writers are called, set out to put the record straight and to make it clear that Jesus had been recognized as the Son of God right from his birth and actually even before his birth. They wrote gospels that focused on Jesus' public career, death, and resurrection, but they added to the basic narrative accounts of his birth. This is an example of Christology, that is, the theology of Christ. The two evangelists wanted to leave no doubt that Jesus had always been the Son of God, and these accounts, which recorded fulfillment of prophecies, signs in the sky, and angelic annunciations, would make that clear. Had the two evangelists not done such Christology, we would never have had Christmas.

But they were writing more than eight decades after the event. How did they know anything about Jesus' birth? As just mentioned, many traditions about Jesus were passed along orally, a common practice of ancient cultures in which very few people could read. It is likely that Jesus' disciples asked him about his early life, and these traditions were passed on in the community. Some common core of traditions survived because Matthew and Luke agree on several basic facts that do not appear in Mark's gospel or any other earlier texts. These include the virginal conception, Jesus' being born in Bethlehem, his father's name being Joseph, and a sign in the sky at the time of his birth. (Mark had already mentioned that his mother's name was Mary and that he grew up in Nazareth.) But the two also disagree on several points, the most important being that in Matthew's gospel Jesus' parents lived in Bethlehem and later moved to Nazareth for the child's safety, while Luke says that they lived in Nazareth and Jesus was born in Bethlehem because his parents had to go there to register for a Roman census. So while we can say that both evangelists knew some common material, they were also uncertain about several specific traditions.

This may be a bit surprising because the ubiquity of crèches, cards, and books about "the first Christmas" give the impression of a continuous, settled narrative, but that does not exist in the New Testament. Matthew speaks of the coming of the Magi, Herod's massacre of the Holy Innocents (the innocent infant boys of Bethlehem), and the Holy Family's flight into Egypt, while Luke tells of the announcement of Jesus' birth to Mary by an angel, of her visit to Elizabeth, of the shepherds visiting the newborn baby, and of the presentation of the child Jesus by his parents in the Temple at Jerusalem. Since the evangelists were not writing their Infancy Narratives for an as yet non-existent feast, they wrote the accounts as introductions to their gospels, which in turn were written for specific early Christian groups. We will understand the infancy narratives best when we realize that the dominant themes of the entire gospels strongly impacted the accounts of Jesus' birth.

THE GOSPEL OF MATTHEW

For generations Christians believed that "Matthew," the author of the first gospel in the New Testament, was one of Jesus' twelve closest disciples, known as the Twelve Apostles. If that were the case, his eye-witness account would be of immeasurable value. But once biblical scholars realized that Matthew had taken large sections of his gospel from Mark, who did not know Jesus personally, they realized that the author of the gospel could not have been one of the Twelve. After all, why would an eyewitness borrow information from someone who did not know Jesus? In that case, who was Matthew?

Possibly from outside the Holy Land, Matthew was a Jewish-Christian, that is, someone who was ethnically Jewish and religiously a Jew but who converted to Christianity, in his case at a time when the new religion was starting to break off from the old one. Matthew wrote for a community that was largely Jewish but was becoming increasingly Gentile. Most likely this community was in the city of Antioch in the Roman province of Syria.

The nature of Matthew's community determined the nature of his gospel. Matthew wanted to explain to his readers who Jesus was and what the church should be, but he also had to deal with Jewish-Gentile tensions. As a Jew, he believed that God's Law as revealed throughout history to his Chosen People was still valid. In his gospel and only in his gospel Jesus says, "I have come not to destroy the Law but to fulfill it" (5:17). But Matthew also believed that the Jewish leaders of Jesus' day had rejected the true Messiah, a mistake which the Jewish leaders of his day were continuing, and so the Christian message went increasingly to Gentiles. Matthew showed the frustration of a believing Jew who believed his people, under poor leadership, were going the wrong way. He presciently accepted that the Gentiles represented the future of Christianity, but he did not want the Jewish element of the new faith to fade. Christianity emerged from Judaism; the life of Jesus was a recent manifestation of the divine activity so evident in the history of Israel. This Jewish-Gentile tension will appear in his Infancy Narrative.

Chapter 1

Matthew's Infancy Narrative appears in chapters 1 and 2 of the gospel, but when we turn to his account of Jesus' birth, we find, to our disappointment, a boring genealogy of "so-and-so begat so-and-so" from Abraham, the father of the Jewish people, down to Jesus, the Messiah. Yet the problem lies not with Matthew but with us. In the ancient Semitic world, you could not really know who people were unless you knew who their ancestors were. To us, this seems unfair. We judge people by who they are, not by who their great-great-grandparents were, but modern attitudes cannot change history. Genealogies make up much of the Old Testament. We do not know about them because no one reads them, either on one's own or from a pulpit—so much better to read about the Exodus or about David and Goliath. But genealogies were so important that the first book of Chronicles devotes its first nine chapters—about a dozen pages in the average modern Bible—to listing how "so-and-so begat so-and-so." As a good Jew, Matthew had to provide a list of Jesus' ancestors. His readers would have found the genealogy important, not boring.

A good example of a biblical genealogy is that of the Jewish hero Ezra. The book named after him lists his ancestry back sixteen generations (Ezra 7:1-5), and the modern reader immediately notes that *all the names are of men*. There is nothing unusual about this. Ancient patriarchal societies considered the man the head of the household and the one who passed on the family name; they thought that it was not important to include the names of the mothers. Matthew follows that path; he is especially concerned to show that Jesus took his descent from David, the greatest of the Jewish kings. But he also includes the names of five women (including Jesus' mother Mary), something shocking for the ancient world. Why?

The answer lies in his belief in the virginal conception of Jesus by Mary before she had come to live with Joseph. Christians accepted that account, but it could be misinterpreted or even manipulated to make Mary look like a sinful woman. Matthew accuses some contemporary Jews of spreading false rumors about Jesus' resurrection (28:11-15), and he worries about possible similar rumors about Mary. This explains the other four women he includes in the genealogy.

The first is Tamar, a Canaanite daughter-in-law of the Hebrew patriarch Judah who had lost three husbands, all sons of Judah, who would not then let her marry his fourth son as tradition demanded. This meant that she would be childless, a disgrace in those days. To avoid this, Tamar posed as a harlot to trick Judah into having relations with her, which he did, and she bore him two sons, one of whom was an ancestor of the great Israelite king David. Judah acknowledged that his devious daughter-in-law had acted more righteously than he did by guaranteeing herself a son (Genesis 38). Next Matthew includes Rahab, another Canaanite and a harlot who helped Joshua's spies plot the conquest of the city of Jericho (Joshua 2). The third woman was Ruth, a Gentile who married a man named Boaz and who became the grandmother of David.

The fourth was the only Jew, Bathsheba, the woman with whom David committed adultery and whose husband, Uriah, he had killed (2 Sam 11–12). Matthew finds her so distasteful that he does not even mention her name, identifying her as "the wife of Uriah," but in spite of her adulterous behavior, she became the mother of the great king Solomon.

By mentioning Mary at the end of the genealogy, Matthew puts her in the company of these women, Gentiles who were by definition outsiders and women who had poor reputations, deserved or undeserved, but, most importantly, women through whom God worked in the history of Israel. Mary may also have been the victim of question and doubt, but Matthew has no question or doubt of Mary's integrity or that God worked through her not just for the good of his Chosen People but for the redemption of the entire human race.

The genealogy also contains some subtle points. Abraham is pre-eminently the father of the Jewish people, but God had also promised him that he would be "the ancestor of a multitude of nations" (Gen 17:4), so this fit Matthew's belief that something that originated with Judaism could spread to other nations just as Abraham's spiritual fatherhood had. Matthew identifies Joseph as the parent who carries Jesus' descent from the great king David, even though Matthew is about to introduce the virginal conception.

How can Joseph carry the Davidic descent if he was not the physical father? Matthew answers the question in verse 1:21, where the angel tells Joseph what to name the baby. According to the Jewish Law, as the biblical scholar Raymond Brown said, "Joseph can acknowledge Jesus by naming him, and that makes him 'son of David,'" something that Jewish-Christian readers would accept as legal fatherhood. (In Luke's gospel, Mary names her son.) Since most Jews believed that the Messiah, the deliverer of Israel, would come from the House of David, Matthew makes it clear that Jesus stands in the Davidic line.

The genealogy has established not only Jesus' ancestral line but also placed him within the history of Israel and, via Abraham, that of other nations as well. It also sets up another Matthean theme, the fulfillment of prophecy which will demonstrate a further link between Jesus and God's Chosen People.

In the rest of chapter 1, Matthew tells us that Mary became pregnant by the Holy Spirit after she was engaged to Joseph, but they did not live together. In ancient Jewish law, such a couple was considered married, even before the consummation of the marriage. She could not keep her pregnancy secret, and Joseph, "a righteous man" (1:19) in the sense of following the Law, was also a kindly man. Although naturally disappointed at his wife's pregnancy, he wanted to dismiss her quietly, sparing her both embarrassment as well as the real chance of her being stoned to death as an adulteress, as in the account of the woman taken in adultery in chapter 8 of John's gospel.

The gospels say very little about Joseph, but this one episode shows him not just to be righteous but also to be someone who can rise above an apparent betrayal and forgive his wife. But then an unnamed angel appeared to Joseph in a dream to comfort him by telling him that Mary conceived miraculously by the Holy Spirit, in fulfillment of a prophecy by the great Jewish prophet Isaiah (7:14) that a virgin would conceive. The angel also told him the child's name, Jesus, while the prophecy adds the symbolic name Emmanuel or "God with us."

In Matthew's Infancy Narrative, God communicates with humans via dreams five times—once to the Magi but four times to Joseph. This recalls for the evangelist's Jewish-Christian readers the Hebrew patriarch Joseph, famous for his interpretation of the dreams of Pharaoh of Egypt. It would also make sense to his Gentile readers since ancient pagans believed that deities contacted people in dreams. Furthermore, events around the birth of Jesus would fulfill five prophecies from the Old Testament, a phenomenon that would carry great weight with Jewish-Christian readers. This introduction to his whole gospel reflects the rest of it. Matthew cites the fulfillment of prophecies throughout Jesus' public career, right down to his Passion.

We see yet another Jewish element in this chapter. The announcement goes to Joseph because according to the Law he was Jesus' legal father and thus the appropriate recipient of this news. Continuing the theme of the virginal conception, Matthew finishes chapter 1 by saying that Joseph did not have relations with his wife before Jesus was born.

Chapter 2

Chapter 2 changes directions as the attention shifts from the Holy Family to the mysterious Magi who suddenly appear, following a star. Contrary to later tradition, Matthew does not say how many Magi there were nor does he give them names or ethnic backgrounds or royal status or even camels to ride on. They are simply *magi*, the plural of the Greek word *magos*, a term widely used of the priests of ancient Babylon and Persia, which is apparently what Matthew means since the Magi came "from the East," and both those kingdoms were east of the Holy Land. The Magi were also astrologers, which is why they left their country to follow a star. Not all biblical references to magi are positive; in the biblical book of Numbers (22–24) Balaam, a *magos* in Jewish tradition, intends to curse the people Israel. Also the word "magic" has the same root as *magos*, a serious concern for Matthew's readers since Jewish law forbade magic.

But these visitors are good magi, and in all good faith they arrive at the court of Herod the Great, king of Judea. Ethnically he was just half-Jewish, and he never took Judaism seriously, practicing it only in public. Politically he was a Roman puppet, and Roman authority guaranteed his long reign (37–4 B.C.). He was a violent, bloodthirsty man, suspicious of all around him. He murdered his wife and three of his sons as well as numerous other innocent people. The Jews hated him— which in turn guaranteed his loyalty to Rome—and Herod returned the hatred. When he knew he was dying, he ordered his surviving son to murder six thousand prominent Jews so that the people would be sorry he had died. Fortunately for the Jews, his son did not follow his father's wishes. [Some readers may have noticed that Herod died in 4 B.C., that is, before the birth of Jesus Christ, which is impossible if Jesus was born during Herod's reign—how can Christ be born before Christ? We will solve that little mystery in chapter 3.]

The Magi seek the newborn "king of the Jews," an important reference by Matthew. He could have called Jesus the Messiah, but Herod's official, Roman-given title was "king of the Jews." By calling Jesus by that name, the Magi have unwittingly alerted Herod to a challenge to his power. The devious king calls his scholars together; they search the holy books; they conclude the Messiah would be born in Bethlehem, thus fulfilling a second prophecy. Herod learns from the Magi when they first saw the star; then he sends them on their way, after first getting them to agree to come back and tell him where the child is so that Herod, too, might go and pay him homage.

The Magi continue their journey, the star leads them to the place where Jesus is, and they go in and give him their now famous gifts of gold, frankincense, and myrrh, all gifts befitting a king. Gold has obvious value; frankincense was used in royal ceremonies; myrrh interestingly enough was used for embalming and has a symbolic importance for Matthew. Next the Magi are warned in a dream, Matthew's second one, not to return to Herod but to go home a different way. Realizing the Magi tricked him, the enraged Herod has his troops kill all the boys in Bethlehem under age two, but, warned by an angel in a dream (Matthew's number three), Joseph takes his wife and son and escapes into Egypt. The flight into Egypt and the massacre of the Holy Innocents fulfill two more prophecies, Matthew's numbers three and four.

Although it may have some historical base, this famous story has problems if taken completely literally. Most obviously, why did Herod not send some spies to follow the Magi to see where the child was? Matthew presents this event as history, but he is obviously working some significant theological themes. As we said earlier, the evangelist was Jewish and lived in a heavily Jewish but increasingly Gentile Christian community. The fulfillment of three more prophecies would appeal to Jewish-Christians, but the real importance lies in the rejection of Jesus by the Jewish leadership in contrast to the faith in Jesus of the Gentile Magi. This foreshadows what would happen at Jesus' death when the leaders of the people turn against Jesus, while the pagan centurion in charge of the crucifixion and some his soldiers publicly acknowledge, "Truly this man was the Son of God" (Matt 27:54).

Since this account also appears in Mark's gospel, Matthew strengthens his account by adding recognition of Jesus' goodness by another Gentile, an account unique to his gospel. The wife of Pontius Pilate is warned *in a dream* that Jesus is an innocent man whom her husband should not harm, but when she tells him so, it is to no avail. Thus Matthew draws a parallel between the beginning and end of Jesus' life. This foreshadowing of Jesus' death would also explain the rather strange gift of myrrh to a baby. Matthew wants to remind his readers how this baby would eventually die to redeem the world. (John's gospel mentions that Jesus' body was wrapped in linen anointed with aloes and myrrh.)

The star makes a second parallel between Jesus' birth and death because at his death other remarkable natural phenomena occurred, such as darkness over all the land and even an earthquake (27:45, 51), and only Matthew among the evangelists mentions these. He may be writing about a baby, but his infancy narrative definitely points toward the Passion.

Matthew also subtly inserts another theme. The Apostle Paul who lived and wrote well before Matthew had said that pagans could recognize the existence of God by looking at the wonders of creation (Rom 1:19-20). Matthew shows the believing Magi moved to adore Jesus by following a natural object, the star, while Herod and his court have God's revealed truth in the form of the Bible, but they are so committed to maintaining their power that they cannot see this truth. And the star plays still another role. In the biblical book of Numbers, the pagan *magos* Balaam prophesies that "a star shall rise out of Jacob" (24:17). Since the patriarch Jacob's other name was Israel, a star rising out of Jacob symbolizes Jesus emerging from the history of Israel, thus reinforcing the genealogy theme. By thus linking the star and the Magi with an ancient Jewish tradition, Matthew has cleverly joined both Jew and Gentile in this story.

The evangelist's concern about his own people causes him to emphasize the purely Jewish element in Jesus' birth narrative. He not only emphasizes that Jesus has indeed fulfilled prophecies and sums up the revelation God had given to his people Israel, but he also casts Jesus in the mold of Moses. Consider the parallel to the infant Moses in the book of Exodus, chapters 1–2. A child is born who can threaten the ruler (Pharaoh=Herod). The ruler attempts to meet the threat by murdering all the boys in the child's community, but the child manages to escape this fate. As an adult Moses had to flee from Egypt; the infant Jesus fled to Egypt.

The Jesus-Moses parallel reappears in the most famous part of Matthew's gospel, the Sermon on the Mount (chs. 5–7), which contains the eight beatitudes and the Lord's Prayer among many other sayings, including the one about Jesus' fulfilling the Law. Just as Moses received the Law on Mount Sinai, so Matthew shows Jesus giving the people the new law on another mount. In addition to the Sermon on the Mount, Matthew's gospel contains four other sizeable discourses by Jesus, and he may have intended them to parallel the five books of the Torah, which Jewish tradition attributed to Moses.

This analysis does not mean that there is no history here; certainly the massacre of the Holy Innocents fits into Herod's character as ancient historians have recorded it. But clearly Matthew's main concern was not history but theology, focusing on themes for both Jewish and Gentile Christians.

Now we return to the Holy Family in Egypt. Matthew gives no indication how long they were there, nor does he say where they stayed. Since there was a large Jewish community in the city of Alexandria, the Holy Family would have fit in there, although the Alexandrian Jews normally used Greek as their daily language. After Herod's death Joseph has a dream (Matthew's number four) in which an angel tells him it is safe to go home, that is, back to Bethlehem, which was in Judea. But when Joseph learns that Herod's son Archelaus now rules Judea for the Romans, he is afraid to go there. Joseph now has Matthew's dream number five in which an angel tells him to go instead to Galilee, a more rural area north of Judea, so this is how the evangelist explains why Jesus was born in Bethlehem but grew up in Nazareth, a town of Galilee. Matthew closes his Infancy Narrative by showing that Jesus' residence in Nazareth fulfills a fifth prophecy.

Biblical scholars will dispute the historical accuracy of several aspects of Matthew's Infancy Narrative, but there can be no dispute about Matthew's literary or theological abilities. He wrote an appealing and sometimes vivid account that brings to life the events surrounding Jesus' birth as an historical event, an act of God, and a continuation of the story of God's Chosen People. This is justly one of the best known stories in the world. Matthew has also demonstrated that for Christians Jesus had always been recognized as the Son of God, his virginal conception accomplished through the Spirit and forecast by an angel in a divinely sent dream. He further demonstrated that, as with his public career, the message of Jesus went first to the Jews, whose leaders opposed him, and now that message will go increasingly to the believing Gentiles, although its Jewish roots will never be abandoned. The evangelist created a superb introduction to his gospel and unknowingly provided half of the base for the one of the greatest feast days his faith would create. The other half would be provided by his contemporary fellow-evangelist, Luke.

THE GOSPEL OF LUKE

With the gospel of Luke, we enter a different world. Although he was a contemporary of Matthew, the two evangelists show no knowledge of one another's work. Luke was most probably a Gentile. He shows little knowledge of Jewish customs but a considerable knowledge of the Eastern Mediterranean Gentile world, that is, the part of the Roman Empire where Christianity first emerged (equivalent to modern Turkey, Greece, Egypt, Lebanon, and Israel), although we cannot say exactly where he lived and wrote. He also places emphasis upon Christianity's message going to the Gentiles.

Luke is the New Testament's great stylist. A conscious literary artist, he raises all his characters to his level. In his writings, everyone from illiterate peasants to Roman governors speak the same good quality Greek. Like all the writers of the New Testament, he wrote for a Christian audience, but he also remained conscious of a larger, educated world. His Infancy Narrative employs several effective literary devices. All this implies a considerable education, which matches the tradition that he was a physician, a title given to him in the Epistle to the Colossians (4:14), although the title might have been symbolic, that is, a physician of souls.

Luke had a great insight. He recognized that the world would not end immediately. Jesus had died a half century before Luke wrote, and he realized that by constantly delaying the Second Coming, God had revealed his true plan, that is, to create the Church. Previously, the Church had functioned as a loose organization to keep the Christians together until the imminent End, but Luke believed that the Church had been established by the Holy Spirit to continue the work of Christ in the world. The Church was a good *in itself*, irrespective of the Second Coming, and so Luke did something no other evangelist did. He wrote a second volume, called the Acts of the Apostles, to recount the work of the Holy Spirit in the Church, especially through the work of Luke's hero, the Apostle Paul.

This second book helps us to understand Luke's gospel and thus his Infancy Narrative. Luke recognized the Jewish rejection of Christianity and the growing movement of the Church into the Roman world. He ended the Acts of the Apostles in Rome when Paul, a prisoner, arrives there for trial. Luke realized that the delayed Second Coming meant that the Christians would have to learn to live with the Romans, and he clearly did not think this was a bad thing. Like almost all Christians, he considered himself a loyal citizen of the empire and did not see Rome and the Church as inevitable enemies.

In the Acts of the Apostles, Roman officials repeatedly save Paul's life when Jewish or pagan mobs threaten it. When Paul is put on trial in Judea, he appeals to Rome, the court of the emperor (at the time Nero), showing Paul's faith in Roman justice. In the gospel (ch. 23) Luke worked overtime to prove that Pontius Pilate, the Roman official who put Jesus to death, was incompetent and cowardly, a man unworthy to be a governor, and so Pilate's judgment against Jesus did not mean that the empire and the faith could not get along. These themes will be strong in the Infancy Narrative.

Many early Christians believed that the Jesus movement should remain part of Judaism or should at least retain many aspects of Jewish law and practice, but Luke, like Paul, belonged to the universalist strain. He believed Christianity to be a faith for all people. Unlike Matthew, Luke did not believe this happened because the Jews did not accept Jesus' message. On the contrary, the message was always intended for people of all ethnic groups, including the Jews whose traditions Luke respected. In his gospel, Luke emphasized how Jesus' message goes to people of all ethnic groups by including the good Samaritan and the centurion who was concerned about a slave. In Acts, many Gentiles welcome Paul's preaching while most Jews challenge it.

But, significantly for the Infancy Narrative, Luke's universalism went beyond ethnic groupings. It also extended to those on the margins of society, such as the poor and the outcast. In the gospel Jesus stays at the house of a notorious tax collector who admits to Jesus that he had cheated people; in response, Jesus says that he came "to seek out and save the lost" (19:1-10). Only Luke tells us that the crucified Lord promised Paradise to one of the thieves who were executed with him. And if the Jewish leaders were glad to get rid of Jesus, the people soon regretted what had happened (23:48). Luke's fondness for the common people appears also in the parable in which the sinful publican is more just than the self-righteous Pharisee (18:9-14).

Yet no marginalized group played such a prominent role in the gospel and Acts as women. Only Luke tells us how Jesus cured the crippled woman (13:10-17), how he raised the widow's son from the dead (7:11-17), and how he enjoyed the company of Martha and Mary (10:38-42), while the Acts of the Apostles speaks of important women converts, such as the businesswoman Lydia (16:11-15). In keeping with the gospel's general approach, women play a major role in the Infancy Narratives, one even more important than that of the men.

Luke was apparently a kindly man because in addition to extending the message to the marginalized and outcasts, whether ethnic or social, he stresses mercy and forgiveness. The publican wins forgiveness for his sins from God (18:9-4), while, on the cross, Jesus forgives those who engineered his death (23:34). This theme too will show up in the Infancy Narrative.

Chapter 1

But when we turn to the first chapter of Luke's gospel, we encounter the same problem that we did with Matthew—where is the Infancy Narrative? In the ancient world, literary figures usually had wealthy patrons who subsidized their work. In an era when books had to be copied by hand, mass marketing was not feasible, and, of course, there were no television or movie deals to be made, and so authors needed patrons. Luke starts off by thanking someone named Theophilus, clearly his patron since this man reappears at the beginning of the Acts of the Apostles. Since the name Theophilus means "one who loves God" in Greek, it may not be a proper name but an honorific one. Luke calls Theophilus "your excellency" which indicates he was an aristocrat, which is what we would expect. Having completed the obligatory dedication, Luke turns to the story.

He starts with an annunciation, yet not one about Jesus but about John the Baptist. Recall that Matthew and Luke wanted to establish that Jesus did not become God's Son after being baptized by John, and Luke will here make the point forcefully. While serving in the Temple in Jerusalem, a Jewish priest named Zechariah sees an apparition of the angel Gabriel. The apparition frightens him, but the angel tells him not to fear and then goes on to forecast that he and his wife Elizabeth would have a son whom they should call John and who would "bring back many of the Israelites to the Lord their God" (1:16). The angel also tells Zechariah that his son "even before his birth would be filled with the Holy Spirit," that is, he would prophesy. Zechariah has doubts because his wife and he are too old to have a child, so the angel gives him a sign of the truthfulness of the message by striking him dumb. When Zechariah returned home from Jerusalem, he had relations with his wife, who conceived.

As the parents of John the Baptist, the last great predecessor of Jesus, Elizabeth and Zechariah fit into a distinct pattern in the Old Testament. God overcame the barrier of advanced age to give a son, Isaac, to Sarah and Abraham, and he also overcame the barrenness of Rebecca, the wife of Isaac, as well as the barrenness of the mother of Samson, and of Hannah, the mother of the Israelite judge Samuel. Thus the universalist Luke is setting his story in the framework of Jewish tradition. [God had to overcome the barrenness of women because in the ancient patriarchal world if a couple did not produce children, it was assumed that the problem was the woman's, never the man's.]

We might expect Luke to continue this story, but instead he switches to a second annunciation story as the angel Gabriel next visits a virgin named Mary who was betrothed to a man named Joseph to tell her that she would become the mother of Jesus.

Before going on with the Annunciation, we should note that Mary lives in Nazareth of Galilee, so here Luke disagrees with Matthew who said that Jesus' parents settled in Nazareth because it was not safe for them to return from

Egypt to Judea. Obviously both evangelists knew that Jesus came from Nazareth but were unsure as to how he got there. This is also proof that Matthew and Luke did not know one another's work because they could have reconciled such an obvious difference.

When we return to the annunciation narrative, we notice a literary device. Luke has paralleled the two annunciations, although with some differences. That is because Luke used a literary device called a step parallel, that is, he paralleled two accounts but one is usually a step higher than the other. A comparison will illustrate this device:

	John the Baptist	*Jesus*
Angel	Gabriel	Gabriel
Human	Zecharaiah	Mary
Son's Name	John	Jesus
Son's Deeds	Bring the Israelites to God	Son of the Most High
	Spirit of Elijah upon him	Have the throne of David
	Many rejoice at his birth	Will have eternal reign
Obstacle	Age of parents	Virginity
Sign	Zechariah struck dumb	Cousin Elizabeth is pregnant

John will be a great man, but Jesus is the Son of the Most High and his reign will have no end. Elizabeth's pregnancy overcame the obstacle of age, a not impossible task (although here accomplished with divine aid), but Mary's pregnancy overcame the obstacle of virginity, a genuinely miraculous occurrence to which the Old Testament offered no parallel. Luke implies that Mary's question to the angel, "How can this come about, since I have no knowledge of man?" was given in a better spirit than Zechariah's because Gabriel punished him for his doubt with the sign of dumbness, while Mary received the good news that her cousin Elizabeth was pregnant with a son and had thus shaken off the disgrace of not having given her husband a male heir. Luke has here advanced a central early Christian theme, the superiority of the mission of Jesus to that of John the Baptist. He has also advanced another of his favorite themes—in his gospel the angel announces Jesus' birth to the woman, not to the man, as happens in Matthew's gospel.

Luke does not tell us much about Mary, but we can deduce some things about her by looking at the historical circumstances. For example, it was common in the ancient world for people to marry as teenagers because life expectancy was so much shorter than today and the chief cause of death for women was childbirth. It was best that a woman become pregnant while healthy and young. Mary was likely fourteen or fifteen years old. It is also likely that she could not read. Few people in the ancient world would "waste" an education on a girl. But society was structured to accommodate the vast majority who could not read, so illiteracy was not the negative it is today. Since parents traditionally chose their children's spouses, we can assume that the marriage of Mary and Joseph was an arranged one, a practice still common in much of the world. Joseph was a carpenter, a craftsman, the kind of husband a small-town girl would have expected. Naturally both husband and wife would have to be Jewish. According to John's gospel, Mary had a sister. That gospel says that "near the cross of Jesus were his mother and his mother's sister. . . ." (19:25), although the other gospels do not mention her.

In an act of kindness, Mary went to visit her cousin Elizabeth. When Elizabeth greeted her, the unborn John jumped in his mother's womb, a sign that he recognized a greater person was there and fulfilling the angel's words to Zechariah that his son would be filled with the Holy Spirit before his birth. His mother Elizabeth also "was filled with the Holy Spirit," so her words to Mary, "Of all women you are the most blessed," have the status of revelation. Luke stresses his point: John and his mother acknowledge the superiority of Jesus and his mother.

Mary next recited a poem, usually called the *Magnificat* from the first word of the Latin translation of the poem, widely used in the Middle Ages when educated people read and spoke Latin. It is a beautiful piece. The nature of the verse proves it was originally created in Greek, and a teenage girl who spoke only the Semitic dialect of Aramaic could not have composed it. Like most ancient authors, Jewish, Greek, and Roman, Luke felt free to put words in the mouths of his characters, and so the *Magnificat* resounds with Lukan themes.

This literary approach does not resonate with modern people who expect authors *not* to put words in people's mouths. But it has good biblical precedents. To give just the most famous example, biblical scholars have shown that the book of Isaiah records not only the prophecies of the great prophet but also of disciples of his who lived hundreds of years later and whose prophecies survive under the prophet's name. These later prophets are known as "Second Isaiah" (chs. 40–55) and "Third Isaiah" (chs. 56–66). Although David did not write all the Psalms, in Jewish tradition all the Psalms went under his name. The ancient Jews also attributed several wisdom writings to the famous king Solomon, even ones like the book of Wisdom which was written in Greek!

In the *Magnificat*, Mary acknowledges that the Lord has "looked upon the humiliation of his servant" but "all genera-tions will call me blessed" (1:48), that is, God chose to work with a humble woman, but he will exalt her through the ages. By working with the lowly, God "has routed the arrogant of heart. He has pulled down princes from their thrones and raised the lowly. He has filled the starving with good things and sent the rich away empty" (1:52-53). Luke does not say that Mary possessed the Holy Spirit when she said these things, but he did not have to. In the ancient world people believed poets to be inspired. And this inspired poet showed God providentially favoring the commoners over the noble, the poor over the rich. Furthermore, Luke's readers who knew the Old Testament would have recognized themes from the great Jewish prophets who also excoriated the aristocracy for their treatment of the lowly, such as Amos who denounced those who "trample on the needy, and bring to ruin the poor of the land" (8:4).

Mary stayed with Elizabeth for three months but left before John was born. When the baby arrived, Zechariah had to write the boy's name on a writing tablet, and when he did, his power of speech returned. He used this newly-regained ability to utter a poem of his own, called the *Benedictus*, again because of its first word in the Latin translation. Like a pious Jew as well as a priest, he praised God for all he had done for his people and then predicted what kind of man John would be. Specifically John "will go before the Lord to prepare a way for him" (1:76). For a pious Jew the Lord was God, but Jesus is frequently called "Lord" in Luke's gospel, and the evangelist's readers would not have missed the point. [A small note here: in verse 1:62 "they began motioning to his father (Zechariah) to find out what name he wanted to give him (the baby)." Why were they motioning rather than speaking? This implies he had been struck deaf as well as mute, although that was not what Luke said the angel had done (1:20). An otherwise careful writer has made a small slip here.]

Luke finishes chapter 1 by telling us that John grew up to be strong and went off to live in the desert until his public career. Saying goodbye to Galilee, Luke turned to a much wider world.

Chapter 2

"In those days a decree went forth from Caesar Augustus that the whole world should be enrolled . . ." (2:1). The geographical change is abrupt, but Luke wants to establish that the birth of Jesus would impact the whole world. When we remember that Luke also wrote the Acts of the Apostles, which ends with the Apostle Paul in Rome, we can see that this Roman setting has great significance for Luke with the Imperial City at the beginning of the gospel and at the conclusion of Acts. Yet the issue is not just Rome but Augustus himself. He was a prince of peace because he put an end to the Roman civil wars and brought order to the Roman world, an achievement with beneficial effects for Christianity (the history of the Church would have been very different if Paul had been murdered by bandits or kidnapped by pirates). Augustus brought peace by successful warfare and by shrewd political manipulation of his opponents; Jesus would bring peace by redeeming humans from sin and reconciling them to God. And the comparison is not just spiritual. Luke loves the idea of comparing the Roman emperor to a poor baby in a frontier province.

As we know, Luke believed that Mary and Joseph lived in Nazareth, and he knew that Jesus was born in Bethlehem, so he had to get the Holy Family there. He did so via the census. He agreed with Matthew that Jesus was born during the reign of Herod (Luke 1:5), but there is no trace of a Roman census in Judea at that time, although there was one about ten years later. Writing eighty years after the events, Luke clearly was uncertain on this issue, but the census allowed him to make an important point at a time when the Christians had to learn to live with Rome: the parents of Jesus were good citizens of the empire, obeying the law to register for the census.

To Bethlehem the Holy Family went, only to find no room in an inn so that they had to take shelter in a stable where Jesus was born. (It is only fair to note that Luke said simply that the inn was full and makes no reference to the rude, unkind innkeeper of later folk and literary tradition.) But without a place to stay in Bethlehem, the Holy Family was symbolically homeless, precursors of the outcast and marginalized that Jesus would preach to in Luke's gospel.

Who were the first ones to recognize the newborn savior? Not educated, important Magi but humble Jewish shepherds, poor, ignorant, odiferous people with whom "proper" people would not want to associate. Yet all was not humble; there was glory there as well. Matthew had a sign in the sky, the star that led the Magi; Luke's sign in the sky was a chorus of angels, letting the shepherds know that Jesus was born, and then uttering the famous and familiar words, "Glory to God in the highest, and peace on earth to men of good will." [This too is a translation of the Latin version, and this passage often appears in liturgical music as the *Gloria*. Actually the Greek text translates, "Glory to God in the highest heaven, and on earth peace among those whom he favors."] The presence of angels not only signifies divine recognition of the newborn child but also reminds us of the angelic apparitions to Zechariah and Mary. Lest we miss the point, Luke uses the

The Grotto of the Nativity from beneath the Basilica of the Nativity in Bethlehem. *Corel Photo.*

same annunciation formula: the angels appear; the shepherds are frightened; an unnamed angel tells them not to fear; a child has been (rather than will be) born; his name is Christ, the Lord; and the sign is that he is lying in the manger.

The shepherds arrived at the stable and venerated the child, telling his parents of the angelic apparition, yet Luke mentions that only Mary kept these things in her heart.

Presumably Joseph was moved as well, but Luke again
focused on the woman.

Obedient to Jewish as well as Roman law, the child's parents
had him circumcised on the eighth day and they gave him the
name Jesus. Luke describes this event very briefly.

He next speaks of the purification of Jesus in the Jerusalem
Temple, once again showing Mary and Joseph acting "in keeping with the Law of Moses" (2:22). This sounds correct, but,
in fact, this Gentile evangelist got it wrong, saying "they" had
to be purified after the birth, when Jewish law required only
that women had to be (Lev 12:2-8). But Luke's real concern is
prophetic recognition of Jesus. Simeon, an "upright and
devout man," was also in the Temple, and "the Holy Spirit
rested upon him," that is, he was a prophet. "Prompted by
the Spirit . . . he took him [Jesus] into his arms and blessed
God and said. . . ." What follows is another Greek poem,
again known by the first words of its Latin translation, the
Nunc Dimittis. Simeon says that this boy will be "a light of
revelation for the Gentiles and glory for (his) people Israel,"
a perfect example of Luke's theology. This boy would glorify
his own people, but his message was for all.

Simeon added another prophecy but this one to Mary. He
warned her that her son was "destined to be a sign that was
opposed" and that "a sword will pierce your soul, too" (2:35).
For generations Christians believed that this meant Mary's
agony at seeing her son on the cross, but this interpretation is
not feasible because in Luke's gospel, Mary is not under the
cross. Only John's gospel places her there (19:25), and that
gospel had not yet been written (it was produced around the
year 100). Most likely the sword symbolized Mary's pain at
having to let Jesus go to do God's work, even at the cost of his
life. This interpretation appears plausible in the next episode,
but first Luke had more to say about the purification.

In addition to Simeon, the prophet Anna also resided in the
Temple. She too prophesied that Jesus would deliver his people.
Women prophets were few but not unknown in ancient

Judaism, for example, the biblical book 2 Kings mentions an important woman prophet named Huldah (22:14), and once again we see Luke emphasizing the role of women in the early life of Jesus and thus symbolically in the life of the Church. He re-emphasizes this point in the Acts of the Apostles where he recorded the presence of women prophets in the early Church, specifically the four daughters of a deacon named Philip (Acts 21:8-9). Luke does not quote any words of Anna but says only that "she spoke of the child to all who looked forward to the deliverance of Jerusalem" (2:38).

Emphasizing again that Jesus' parents did "everything that the Law of the Lord required," Luke tells us they returned to Nazareth. When Jesus was twelve, his parents took him to Jerusalem for Passover. When the feast was over and they joined the other pilgrims on the road home, Mary and Joseph realized that Jesus was not with them. They checked with relatives and friends but could find him nowhere. They went back to Jerusalem where they found him three days later—a symbol of the Resurrection when Jesus was gone but returned in three days—in the Temple where he was debating theology with the resident wise men and impressing them with his knowledge and intelligence. When Mary, and not Joseph, asked him why he put his parents through such agony, he replied that he must do what his Father, that is, God, requires. For the first time—but not the last—Mary's soul is pierced with a sword, her anguish over a lost child taking second place to the demands of his mission.

Luke closes his account by telling us that Jesus lived with his parents and continually "increased in wisdom, in stature, and in favor with God and with people" (2:52).

THE GOSPEL ACCOUNTS AND HISTORY

Like Matthew, Luke has given us a fine account, replete with tenderness (the elderly Elizabeth and Zechariah finally able to have a son), with superb poetry, with effective literary devices, and an important Christology. But how historical is his account, or rather, how historical can either or both gospel accounts be?

First, we must in all fairness remember that both evangelists wrote eighty to ninety years after the event and did not have access to reliable written sources, only to oral traditions passed along for decades, and even then only to the oral traditions known to their own local communities. We should not be surprised that they disagree on some points, although they also agree on several points.

The one unambiguous fact upon which both agree is that Jesus was born during the reign of Herod the Great. Luke adds the reign of Caesar Augustus (31 B.C.–14 A.D.), which is historically accurate since Herod and Augustus were contemporaries.

There is no doubt that Jesus was born in Bethlehem and that his father was Joseph, details not found in Mark or other writings earlier than these two gospels. It seems plausible that his parents lived in Nazareth before his birth because Matthew's explanation depends upon Herod's massacre of the innocent children, and since that fits the evangelist's comparison of Jesus to Moses, it is less historically probable than Luke's account. On the other hand, Luke's explanation of the birth in Bethlehem because of a census falters for a lack of evidence for such a census at that time and coincides perhaps too well with his obvious desire to place Jesus' birth in a Roman setting.

Matthew says nothing about John the Baptist. Luke's claim that he was Jesus' cousin does not reappear in his gospel's account of the two as adults, a puzzling omission if his Infancy Narrative is historically accurate on this point. Luke is the only source for the names of John's parents.

Since both evangelists wrote about the virginal conception, the tradition clearly antedated both of them and was authoritative, yet it has been the topic of some questioning because the Hebrew version of Isaiah 7:14 does not read "virgin" but rather "young woman." Over the centuries, this has led to suspicion and sometimes the accusation that the evangelists

changed the text to accommodate Christian teaching. But
that is simply untrue. In the centuries before Jesus was born,
many Jews migrated to the city of Alexandria in Egypt, a
Greek-speaking locale. These immigrants soon began to
speak Greek and wanted a translation of the Bible in that
language. When the Jewish translators got to Isaiah, they
translated "young woman" with the Greek word for "virgin."
Thus the Christian evangelists cited a *Jewish* edition of
Isaiah; they did not change the text.

Even if Luke does get a few things wrong, his portrayal of
Jesus' parents as faithful, practicing Jews is accurate because
the adult Jesus is at home in synagogues and can debate the
Law with learned Jews, as he does as a boy in Luke's gospel.
Jesus clearly grew up in a pious household. Matthew supports
the notion of the boy's piety by telling us that Joseph was a
righteous man, that is, one who followed the Law, and so we
can expect him to have brought up his son to know and
follow the Law.

Both writers include a sign in the sky, and both also intend
it to be miraculous. Luke speaks unequivocally about angels,
while Matthew speaks of a star that moves and which leads
the Magi to Jesus (clearly not just a normal star). But it is
significant that both mention a heavenly sign; clearly a
tradition about that existed. Furthermore, as the appendix
to this chapter shows, some modern astronomers believe
there was a stellar phenomenon that could explain
this tradition.

An agreement upon the names of Jesus' parents, the places
of his birth and childhood, the ruling monarchs, and miraculous elements such as the virginal conception and the sign in
the sky may not seem like much to a modern historian, but
they represent far more than we know about many other great
figures of Antiquity, Greek, Jewish, Egyptian, or Roman. More
importantly, we must recall that the historical setting is just
that—a setting in which Matthew and Luke recounted how
they, as believing Christians, understood Jesus.

APPENDIX: THE STAR

For generations astronomers have tried to identify the Star of Bethlehem, but with the rise of modern biblical study in the nineteenth century, religion scholars have downplayed the reality of the star in favor of a symbolic or theological explanation, such as the star rising out of Jacob or the parallel to the sign in the sky (the darkening) at Jesus' death. For such scholars, Matthew clearly did not intend his star to be understood as a physical reality.

But if that is the case and if Matthew simply fabricated the story of the star and the Magi to show Gentiles accepting Jesus while the Jewish leadership try to harm him, then we have to ask why did Matthew choose this particular story? He could have made up anything to show Gentile acceptance. And why not use Romans or Greeks to represent the Gentiles? They would have been much more familiar to his congregation than the magi "from the East." And why use a star? Plenty of other natural phenomena could come to mind, especially when we recall that when Matthew was writing in the 80s, the eruption of Mount Vesuvius and the destruction of Pompeii in 79 were fresh in people's minds. For that matter, why does he need natural phenomena at all to show the Gentiles' acceptance of Christ? Unanswered questions like these convinced some modern astronomers that there was likely a good historical reason why Matthew chose an astral phenomenon.

Modern astronomers have "walked down the hall," so to speak, and talked with their colleagues in the religion department. They understand that Matthew had a theological rather than an historical theme in mind, but they still believe that some astral event occurred about the time Jesus was born that convinced Matthew to use a star for his symbolism. If the astronomers are correct, then it is possible that Matthew not only made a theological point but also passed along an historical tradition.

This writer is not an astronomer and cannot evaluate the scientific questions involved, but readers who want to know more about this topic should consult two books written for a general audience, *The Star of Bethlehem: An Astronomer's View* by Mark Kidger (1999) and *The Star of Bethlehem: The Legacy of the Magi* by Michael Molnar (2000). Both writers did their historical homework, and they pay great attention to how the ancient Magi understood the stars because it is not enough to prove that some astral phenomenon existed—that goes on all the time—but rather that some phenomenon occurred that was so grand or so unique that it moved people to believe that some great event had occurred on earth.

They argue that ancient astrologers would look not just to one event in the sky but to several, because multiple events made interpretation more reliable and the astrologers did not have to bet everything on interpreting one event correctly. The modern astronomers believe that several events did occur in the period 6 to 4 B.C., such as a conjunction of planets in the constellation Pisces (Kidger) or Aries (Molnar), a further massing of planets in Pisces, followed by two pairings in the same constellation, and finally a supernova observed by Chinese astronomers in 5 B.C. and by Korean astronomers in 4 B.C. Kidger believes that the Star of Bethlehem might be a star called DO Aquilae, but concedes that "it would be quite astonishing if this turns about to be correct. Most likely it is some other, now anonymous star. . . ."

The physical star may not have been the evangelist Matthew's central concern, but modern astronomers make a good case for some unique astral phenomenon or phenomena at the time of Jesus' birth.

CHAPTER TWO

Creating the Christmas Story

By the year 125, when the last books of the New Testament had been written, most Christians had accepted Luke's belief that the world would not end soon and the Second Coming of Christ was off in an indefinite future. To be sure, many fringe groups, then and now, claimed that the end was near, but the majority of Christians have accepted that they will be citizens of this world for some time and that they should learn to get along in it.

In the second century that meant that the Christians had to organize their assemblies and churches for day-to-day living. The literature of the period shows fewer and fewer references to prophets and charismatic figures and more and more references to those engaged in day-to-day ministries, people perhaps not as compelling as prophets but more necessary to keep the Church functioning. One of the organizing tendencies of the second century was the attempt to determine if there was a specifically Christian collection of inspired books. The Christians answered in the affirmative, and church leaders began the task of deciding which books were inspired or, to phrase it a bit differently, which ones belonged in a *canon*.

Canon is a Greek word meaning a "ruler" or "measuring stick," and it came to mean a standard of judgment. When Jews and Christians spoke of the canon of Scripture, they meant those books that met the standard of judgment for divine inspiration, and the canon now means the list of books contained in the Bible. The second-century Christians wondered if a book should be included because of its author, such as Paul, or its content, such as accounts of Jesus, or its continuous use in particular churches, such as that of the Apocalypse in western Asia Minor or some combination of these. It would take the Christians until the fourth century to finalize the canon, but by the late second century they had decided that four accounts of Jesus, and only those four, belonged in the canon. These books are the now accepted gospels of Matthew, Mark, Luke, and John. Thus from the second century onward, Christians regarded the two gospels containing the story of Christ's nativity as inspired Scripture, which guaranteed that the stories would never be lost and would always play an important role in the understanding of Jesus. His nativity may not have been very important in the first century, and it may take up but four chapters in only two gospels, but it was here to stay.

The phrase "only those four" gospels may have surprised some readers. Are there not only four gospels? Not at all. Because these four found acceptance in the Bible, the others have passed from the religious horizon, but in fact there were about two dozen gospels in the ancient Church. Today all these gospels along with many other books fall under the heading of *New Testament Apocrypha*.

The apocryphal Scriptures are books which claim to be by or about biblical figures, but which have not been accepted into the canon. Our concern will be the Christian apocryphal infancy narratives, but there were also Jewish apocryphal books. Have you ever wondered what happened to Eve and Adam after God expelled them from the Garden of Eden? Then read *The Life of Adam and Eve*. Do most of the twelve sons of Jacob seem rather colorless and dull? Then read *The Testaments of the Twelve Patriarchs*, and learn their views on a variety of matters. Jewish apocryphal literature includes histories, prophecies, and psalms. Christian apocryphal literature also mimics the Bible and includes gospels, acts of apostles, epistles, and apocalypses.

The earliest Christian apocryphal books, those of the second century, present some intriguing problems. Do they contain any reliable history? For example, one prominent apocryphal book we will soon be looking at contains the names of Jesus' maternal grandparents, Joachim and Anna. Are these their real names? We know from the Acts of the Apostles by Luke that Mary was with her son's disciples after his death. She could have told them something about her family, and this material was preserved orally for generations. There is no reason why a non-biblical book could not contain reliable historical information, but such supposed information must be used very carefully.

Why were the apocryphal books written? No one answer presents itself because many people wrote such works, and they had their own diverse reasons. Often a particular Christian group wanted to push its distinctive views and tried to justify them by putting them in a book supposedly written by some biblical figure. At other times people simply wrote imaginative accounts that reflect the influence of folklore upon the new and developing religion. Possibly the writers recorded some information that they thought to be historically accurate.

The interest in the infancy of Jesus reflects the Christian awareness of being in the world for some time. The very first Christians, who expected Jesus to return on clouds and in power at any moment, had little interest in history, which was, after all, about to end. But second-century Christians realized that they would be part of history, and consequently they took an increasing interest in Jesus' "history," that is, his earthly life. Thanks to the canonical gospels, they knew much of his public career and his death but next to nothing about his infancy and childhood. To use a modern image, the demand was there and just waiting for people to take it up.

The apocryphal infancy gospels did not detract from the gospel accounts but rather added to them. Early Christians accepted the basic Infancy Narratives; they simply wanted more. At the same time they were turning to the apocrypha for information, they were also turning to a much older source, the Old Testament, and we will look there first.

As we saw with Matthew's gospel, the Christians looked to the Old Testament for prophecies that the life of Christ had fulfilled. Matthew had found five prophecies of the Nativity, yet surely, the Christians believed, there must be more. But how to find them? The best way was to look for some key word in the Infancy Narratives and see if it occurs in any appropriate biblical text. One such biblical verse would forever change our visual portrayal of Christmas.

The ox and the donkey. Sarcophagus (fourth century).
Pio Cristiano Museum, Rome.

The Christians cited the prophet Isaiah more than any other, and when they turned to him, they found a major reference right in the beginning of his book. Isaiah was reproaching the people Israel for not obeying the Lord: "I reared the children and brought them up, but they have rebelled against me. The ox knows its owner and the donkey its master's manger, but Israel does not know, my people does not understand" (Isa 1:2-3). The key word, of course, is "manger," a link to the gospel of Luke (2:7). Identifying the "master" in the prophecy as Christ, Christians took the reference about the ox and the donkey and applied it to the Infancy Narrative. This approach caught on quickly, and ever since the second century our picture of the birth of Jesus, reflected in much art and countless crèches in churches and homes, has included an ox and a donkey. So familiar is this picture, that most people who read the Infancy Narratives are surprised to find that the ox and donkey are not mentioned there.

Although the legends of the Magi developed rather late, not really until the fifth century, they also derived imagery from the prophetic books, especially Isaiah. That book forecast a wonderful future for Jerusalem, but one image it used convinced the early Christians that the verses really applied to Christ: "A multitude of camels shall cover you, the young camels of Midian and Ephah; all those from Sheba shall come. They shall bring gold and frankincense and shall proclaim the praise of the Lord" (Isa 60:6). Whatever the original meant, for the Christians the phrase "they shall bring gold and frankincense" had to refer to the Magi, even if the myrrh were left out. But even if that were so, what does this verse add to the Infancy Narrative? Look at the opening words of the verse. The people bringing these gifts traveled by camel, as almost every image of the Magi has shown them to do, even though Matthew's gospel does not mention how they traveled.

But this Isaian chapter had even more to offer. At verse 3 it says that "nations shall come to your light, and the kings to the brightness of your dawn," while verses 10 and 11 speak about foreign kings ministering to Jerusalem—or Christ as the Christians now interpreted this verse—and about his reception of the wealth of nations with kings in attendance. Yet when did kings ever come to Christ? The gospels mention nothing like that. But in the Bible the word "nations" means the Gentiles, and verse 10 had spoken about foreign kings. The Christians put all this together and realized that the only foreigners who came to Christ bearing gifts and ministering to him were the Magi. These Isaian verses would play a role in turning the magi into kings, as we shall see in chapter 4.

Putting all this together, we can say that, starting in the second century, Christian interpretation of Old Testament helped to create a new and fuller Christmas story, one that was expanded in the centuries that followed.

PROTOEVANGELIUM OF JAMES

The oldest apocryphal infancy gospel bears the name the *Protoevangelium of James*, the suffix "proto" to show that it is the first gospel, the earliest good news. Today we would call it a "prequel" because it purports to tell the story of Jesus' parents, and particularly of his mother, before the gospel accounts. The "James" of the title is not identified in the text, but he probably is supposed to be the James who is so prominent in the Acts of the Apostles as leader of the Jerusalem community. He was a good choice as the supposed author because Acts identifies him as "the brother of Jesus" and thus someone who was knowledgeable about the early history of Mary and Joseph. The *Protoevangelium* originated in Syria and dates to the mid-second century. In general, Syrian Christians had a great interest in Mary and especially in emphasizing her virginity, as this "gospel" will show.

It starts with the birth of Mary. Her father Joachim, a rich man, and his wife Anna could have no children. As usual, the fault was the woman's. An angel of the Lord appeared to Anna to tell her she would conceive, and she promised to give the child to the Lord. This account parallels not only the Lucan Infancy Narrative but also the biblical story of the judge Samuel whose mother Hannah (the Hebrew form of Anna) could not have children until the Lord intervenes, and she and her husband gave the child to serve in the local shrine at Shiloh. So happy was Hannah that she had conceived that she burst into poetry rather similar to Mary's

Magnificat (1 Sam 1–2). It is possible that the author of this gospel got the name Anna from Hannah.

Joachim and Anna gave Mary to the Temple when she was three; while there, she received food from the hand of an angel, proof that God was with her. But when she turned twelve, that is, when she was old enough to menstruate, the male elders of the Temple decided to marry her off before she polluted the sacred environment, a classic patriarchal fear. The method for selecting a husband was revealed by an angel to the priest Zechariah, the future father of John the Baptist, a clever reworking of a biblical account. Local widowers were invited to bid for Mary's hand, and one of those was Joseph. When the widowers came to the Temple, they were given rods. The high priest prayed, and suddenly a dove emerged from Joseph's rod and flew onto his head, proving that he was the divinely designated husband for Mary as well as recalling for Christian readers the Holy Spirit, thus proving that God chose Joseph. The canonical gospels say nothing of this fanciful event.

But the *Protoevangelium of James* uses this account in order to address a major problem for the Syrian Christians, namely, the brothers of Jesus who appear several times in the gospels, e.g., Matthew 12:46, Mark 3:31, and one of whom, James, is the supposed author of this gospel. The Syrians believed that Mary was always a virgin, and so they had to explain who Jesus' brothers were. Modern churches that believe in Mary's perpetual virginity teach that "brothers" is a more general designation for blood relatives such as cousins, a valid interpretation of the word, but the ancient Syrians took a different tack. Joseph declines to take Mary as his wife because "I already have sons and am old." The *Protoevangelium* has already told us that Joseph was a widower, and now we learn that he had sons. These were the "brothers" of Jesus, that is, the sons of his legal if not biological father and thus legally his stepbrothers. The reference here to Joseph's being old will explain something else, namely, why in so many medieval and Renaissance paintings of the Nativity, Joseph appears as an old man. The *Protoevangelium* may not have made it into the New Testament canon, but it has influenced a traditional visual portrayal of Christmas.

The Temple elders convinced Joseph to take Mary into his house, but he declined to marry her, insisting instead on caring for her and protecting her virginity. This differs from the gospels, which say that they were husband and wife, but the *Protoevangelium of James* wants to play down any marital contact between the two. The Syrian Christians wanted to avoid any hint that Mary and Joseph might have had marital relations so they simply eliminate any mention that the two were ever married, even though by doing so they actually contradict the gospels.

Joseph set Mary up in his house and then left her for some months. No longer the humble carpenter of the gospels, he had become a general contractor, and he went off to build his buildings. When he returned, he concluded that she had betrayed his trust, had an affair with someone, and became pregnant. He compared his deception to that of Adam and, assuming Mary had been seduced, compared her deception to that of Eve. At the same time the *Protoevangelium* was being composed, Christian theologians had begun to identify Mary as the New Eve, just as the Apostle Paul had called Jesus the New Adam. The Mary-Eve parallel became very popular in the early Church.

Mary insisted that she was a virgin, but Joseph did not believe her. Being the righteous man of Matthew's gospel, he decided to put her away quietly, until an angel appeared to him and assured him that Mary had told him the truth. But the angelic appearance has an important detail. In Matthew's gospel, the angel says, "Do not be afraid to take Mary home *as your wife* because that which is in her is of the Holy Spirit" (1:20), but in the *Protoevangelium* the angel says, "Do not be afraid because of this child because that which is in her is of the Holy Spirit." This is not an error; as we just saw, the author of this text will ignore Scriptures—in this case, change the angel's words—to prevent hints of contact between Mary and Joseph.

Joseph as an old man in Renaissance art. Detail, *The Flight into Egypt* by Guido Reni, 17th century. *Bradford City Art Gallery.*

But Mary's pregnancy could not be hidden forever. The Jerusalem high priest and the Temple elders learned of it and reproached both her and Joseph, who insisted on their innocence. The elders demanded a trial by ordeal. Mary and Joseph had to drink something the writer calls "the water of conviction," which would somehow reveal their sin. They drank the water, nothing happened, and the high priest declined to condemn them, using the words Jesus used to the accused sinful woman in John's gospel (8:11): "If the Lord God has not made manifest your sins, neither do I condemn you."

While Joseph was away, Mary had gone to visit Elizabeth. The *Protoevangelium* includes no poetry by either of them, but it does add the detail that Mary was sixteen years old. The anonymous author probably made a conjecture about Mary's age, but it is a logical one, given the usual age for girls to be married in the ancient world. As late as the fifth century, the average age for a first-time bride in the city of Rome was twelve. This conjecture was also to have a long future. Most artistic portrayals of Mary show her in her mid-teenage years rather than as an adult.

The *Protoevangelium* also determined what would become a popular and enduring approach to Christmas. The anonymous author combined the two Infancy Narratives and simply overlooked the discrepancies, for example, Joseph's intent to put Mary away quietly is from Matthew (1:19) while the visit to Elizabeth is from Luke (1:39-56). This is now common, for example, most Christmas crèches in both churches and private homes blend the two stories.

Next we read that a decree had gone forth from "king" Augustus to enroll the whole world. Joseph did not know how to enroll Mary because, unlike the Joseph of the canonical gospels, he was not her husband in this account. He even debated enrolling her as his daughter, but he would not lie. When they went off to Bethlehem, they did not go alone. One of Joseph's sons led their donkey, so the *Protoevangelium* here adds a human character to the story but also an animal, the donkey, which we saw in the book of Isaiah.

The author abandons the no-room-in-the-inn account because Mary gave birth in a cave before they even got to Bethlehem. This is the first mention of the cave, which would become a regular feature of medieval Christmas stories. Joseph, understandably concerned, went looking for a midwife. When the midwife arrived, she had doubts about Joseph's story, but when she saw the cave filled with a bright light, she burst into her own version of the *Magnificat*. After the baby's birth, the midwife told her friend Salome about a virgin birth—not a virginal conception but a virgin *birth*, that is, the baby arrived without any changes to the mother's body. Salome doubted this and said, "Unless I put forward my finger and test her condition, I will not believe that a virgin brought forth." This situation reflects the story of the Doubting Thomas of John's gospel, the disciple of Jesus who would not believe that the Lord has risen from the dead unless he put his hand into Jesus' side (John 20:24-29).

Mary agreed to Salome's rather coarse proposal. Salome performed the act and then cried out, "Woe for my wickedness and my unbelief." God immediately punished Salome for her unbelief by withering her hand, only to restore it when she repented. This story became extremely popular, and it helped to foster the doctrine that Mary was a virgin before the birth, *during* the birth, and after the birth. The canonical gospels speak of the virginal conception, thus making Mary a virgin before the birth, and by the fourth century most Christians believed that she maintained her virginity after the birth. On the surface, the doctrine of Mary's perpetual virginity would mean simply that she and Joseph were never physically intimate. The author of the *Protoevangelium*, however, defined virginity in a wider sense, that is, as including the physical integrity of the body. This extended definition of virginity was taken up by several prominent ancient theologians, although without the baggage of the entire *Protoevangelium*. These theologians applied it to the doctrine of Mary's perpetual virginity, and it was adopted by medieval church councils and has become part of official Roman Catholic teaching about Mary, although not of other Western churches.

After the midwife and Salome, the Magi appeared next. The only change the *Protoevangelium* has introduced to the gospel account is to heighten the magnificence of the star. The Magi, still unnamed and unnumbered, told Herod, "We saw how an indescribably greater star shone among the other stars and dimmed them, so that they no longer shone." This, too, had a long pictorial future; think of how many Christmas cards you have seen with a huge, very bright star being followed by the wise men. After the Magi's visit and the Holy Family's flight into Egypt, the Infancy Narrative ends.

But the *Protoevangelium* adds another brief story. One of the children whom Herod's soldiers sought to kill was John the Baptist. Fortunately for him a mountain opened up and hid John and his mother Elizabeth inside. But Zechariah did not fare as well. Herod's henchmen found him and killed him. Zechariah's place in the Temple was taken by Simeon, who would prophesy about Jesus when his parents brought him to the Temple. This anecdote shows the problem of conflating the two gospel stories. How can Simeon prophesy about Jesus in the Temple (Luke) when his parents had already fled to Egypt (Matthew)? We will never know because the author of the *Protoevangelium* simply glossed over the problem and ended his very entertaining and influential gospel.

INFANCY GOSPEL OF THOMAS

Also from second- or third-century Syria is the *Infancy Gospel of Thomas,* an anonymous work that claims authorship by one of Jesus' twelve apostles. The book actually does not deal with Jesus' birth but his childhood. Thanks to the gospel of John, Christian belief in Jesus' divinity had become well-established by the second century. This quickly led to the belief that he had always had divine powers, which he must have used as a child. This defines divinity rather shallowly, but in the ancient world the visible demonstration of power counted for much. The problem with the *Infancy Gospel of Thomas* lies less with notions of power than with the manifestations of it. This book portrays Jesus as a detestable little brat who uses his power to punish people who run afoul of him. When a boy bumps into him, he strikes the boy dead. When the boy's parents complain to Joseph, he upbraids Jesus for his behavior. Jesus replies, "I know that these words are not yours; nevertheless for your sake I will be silent. But these people (the parents) shall bear their punishment." He then inflicts blindness upon them. This infuriates Joseph who grabs Jesus' ear and wrings it very hard. The angry Jesus turns on Joseph and warns him, "Don't you know that I am not your child? Don't vex me!" Not surprisingly, this "gospel" was never a serious candidate for the New Testament canon.

Jesus does do some good things in this book, such as raising a young man from the dead, but generally the *Infancy Gospel of Thomas* paints an appalling picture of him. Yet it does demonstrate the growing Christian interest in Jesus' childhood as well as the increasing intrusion of folklore elements into stories of that childhood.

ARABIC INFANCY GOSPEL

Some other early works have not survived, but some ancient writers quoted fragments of them. A third-century Roman Christian named Hippolytus quoted a lost gospel that tells of angels appearing to Jesus at age twelve to instruct him about what had happened to the world since the Garden of Eden as well as what would happen in the future. The reference to Jesus' age clearly refers to how he amazed the Temple elders with his learning, so now we know where he got all that knowledge!

In several cases some early works survive in later manuscripts, that is, the original books have disappeared and only later copies survive, so that scholars cannot be sure of the exact date of the book's composition. A work called the *Arabic Infancy Gospel* is what it name suggests, an infancy gospel preserved in the Arabic language. It originated probably in the fourth or fifth century. Famous in the Middle East, it included the prophet Mohammed among those who knew its traditions, and some of its legendary material appears in the Koran. This gospel focused on what the Holy Family did in Egypt. Matthew says only that they went there but nothing about what they did there. Although artistic representations of the event show the Holy Family with the pyramids in the background, Matthew probably meant that they went to Alexandria, which had a large Jewish community. There they would have fit in easily and presumably Joseph could have found work—if indeed the story is historically accurate and not just part of Matthew's attempt to parallel Moses and Jesus.

Miracles abound. When Mary had washed the baby Jesus, she poured some of the bath water upon a girl who had leprosy. This symbolic baptism immediately cured the girl. But not all of the Holy Family's adventures were happy ones. Crossing a desert by night, they were captured by two robbers, part of a much larger band. One robber, Titus, told the other one, Dumachus, that they should let these good people go before the other robbers discovered them and harmed them. Dumachus refused, so Titus ransomed the Holy Family by giving Dumachus forty drachmae. This moved the infant Jesus to tell his mother, "In thirty years, mother, the Jews will crucify me in Jerusalem, and those two robbers will be fastened to the cross with me, Titus on my right hand and Dumachus on my left. After that day, Titus will go before me into paradise."

This story parallels many ancient romance tales that separated characters—often brothers and sisters at birth—only to have them meet again decades later. It certainly is an intriguing motif, the infant Jesus meeting the two men with whom he would later die, but this tale also offers some sound theology. Like Matthew's gospel, it links the Nativity of Jesus with his passion, a theme that survived until Christmas became primarily a children's holiday in the nineteenth century. The theme even survives in some Christmas carols of that century, for example, in "We Three Kings of Orient Are" (written in 1865) the king who brings the myrrh sings "Sorrowing, sighing, bleeding, dying/Sealed in the stone cold tomb." We also see that although Jesus says that Titus will go to paradise, he says nothing about Dumachus. This adheres to official Christian teaching that refuses to name a single person who is actually in hell, despite the tendency of individual Christians, such as the great medieval Italian poet Dante, to name quite a few of those who are there.

GOSPEL OF PSEUDO-MATTHEW

About the year 800, an anonymous Latin author collected a group of ancient traditions into a work now known as the

Gospel of Pseudo-Matthew. This vivid account achieved great popularity in the Middle Ages.

Pseudo-Matthew (as we must call the author) starts off with the birth of Jesus, citing Isaiah for the ox and the donkey, but also adding a quotation from another Old Testament prophet, Habbakuk, who said, "Between two beasts you are known" (3:2). Actually, the original Hebrew does not say that, but Pseudo-Matthew read the book of Habbakuk in an erroneous Latin translation of an older Greek translation. Since few people in the Middle Ages could read either Hebrew or Greek (or, for that matter, could read at all), Pseudo-Matthew did not question his source, and medieval Christians came to assume that Habbakuk had also prophesized the ox and the donkey.

Like the author of the *Arabic Infancy Gospel*, Pseudo-Matthew realized the dramatic possibilities of expanding upon the Holy Family's stay in Egypt. When dragons threaten them, Jesus pacifies the monsters. He urges his parents not to worry since he has power over all beasts, and, sure enough, "lions and leopards worshipped him and accompanied them in the desert." Pseudo-Matthew here follows the Apostle Paul who called Jesus the new Adam. The human race is now back in the Garden of Eden where people and wild animals could live in harmony, a good theological point. As Pseudo-Matthew points out, it fulfilled a prophecy, a very famous one: "The wolf and the lamb shall feed together; the lions shall eat straw like the ox" (Isa 65:25). The fulfillment of prophecy proves that the author of Pseudo-Matthew had read the original Matthew carefully.

Jesus shows his power not only over animals but also over pagan gods. When the Holy Family arrives at the town of Hermopolis, for some reason these pious Jews go into a pagan temple. When they do, all the idols fall on their faces and break in pieces, which Pseudo-Matthew claimed fulfilled yet another prophecy of Isaiah (19:1). The local Egyptian governor rushes to the temple with his entire court to avenge this impiety, but when he gets there and sees all the idols on the

ground, he immediately recognizes Jesus' divinity. He also
warns his troops that if they try to harm this child, they will
be destroyed as was Pharaoh's army in the Red Sea, another
linking of Jesus and Moses, just as the canonical Matthew
had done. Shortly after this, an angel tells Joseph that the
Holy Family could return to the Holy Land.

Pseudo-Matthew also tells a story that metamorphosed
over time and became a staple of Christmas music in England,
although less so in North America. Weakened by the intense
Egyptian sun, Mary tells Joseph she needs to rest. Looking at
a fruit-laden tree, she says, "I wish someone could get me
some of these fruits." Joseph points out that they are well
beyond his reach and, besides, they need water more than
fruit. The infant Jesus, however, orders the tree to bend over
so that his mother can have some fruit. He also arranges for
water to flow from the base of the tree.

The beautiful English hymn "The Cherry Tree Carol" dates
from the Late Middle Ages, and the wording first appeared in
1696. The scene is not Egypt but Galilee shortly after the
annunciation to Mary but before the angel told Joseph what
was happening. The two are walking together in a cherry
orchard. Mary asks,

> "Pluck me one cherry, Joseph,
> For I am with child.
> Then bespoke Joseph
> With answer most unkind,
> 'Let him pluck thee a cherry
> That brought thee now with child.'"

The carol then attributes to Jesus a pre-natal miracle:

> "O then bespoke the baby
> Within his mother's womb,
> 'Bow down then the tallest tree
> For my mother to have some.'"

The tree obeys Jesus; Mary has her fruit; Joseph realizes
that "I have done Mary wrong." There is no way to trace pre-

cisely the development of the legend from Pseudo-Matthew to the carol, although the basic lines are there. But Pseudo-Matthew has prescinded from the biblical gospel, while the carol contradicts it. In Matthew's account, an angel tells Joseph not to distrust Mary even though she is pregnant, while in the carol he learns that this is a miraculous pregnancy when the unborn child speaks from the womb and does a miracle. Actually, pre-natal miracles appear frequently in medieval saints' lives. In Irish tradition St. Patrick saved his mother from poisoning before he was born. All such stories derive from Luke's Infancy Narrative where John the Baptist jumps in the womb at the presence of Jesus.

APOCRYPHAL INFANCY ACCOUNTS AND THEOLOGICAL MOTIFS

Some apocryphal infancy accounts have very specific theological motifs that became generally accepted by the larger Church, such as the new Adam motif via the Garden of Eden comparisons, but some accounts represent the views of groups that simply disappeared over the centuries. At the end of the first century, the Christians converted more and more Gentiles, most of them Greek-speaking and with traditional Greek views on life. Since the Church was emphasizing Jesus' divinity, some of these converts wondered how a divine being could become incarnate because a divine being was purely spiritual, the very antithesis of the flesh. Furthermore, the spiritual existed free of the corruptions of the flesh, and these Gentiles considered it unworthy that the Son of God had taken on a body.

But that raised an obvious and serious problem: people had seen Jesus in the flesh as the gospels and other traditions recorded. Well, not exactly, was the reply. Jesus did not have a real body, he only *seemed* to have body. The Greek word for "seem" is *dokéo*, and so Christians who believed Jesus only appeared to be physical came to be called "docetists." Docetism never became a formal movement but was rather a widely-shared attitude. Its adherents believed that if you tried to touch Jesus, your hand would go right through his body. He was not a complete human being but rather a phantom. This approach had no future in Christianity because right from the time of the Apostle Paul Christians had emphasized that Jesus redeemed the human race from sin and death by his suffering, death, and resurrection, all of which were impossible if he did not have a true body. But docetism could still exercise some influence.

LATIN INFANCY GOSPEL IN THE ARUNDEL MANUSCRIPT

In a work from the fourth or fifth century called the *Latin Infancy Gospel in the Arundel Manuscript*, named for the British Museum manuscript in which it is preserved, we see docetic tendencies. The midwife reappears as does the cave as Jesus' birthplace. The midwife speaks in the first person and recounts the nativity. "The maiden [Mary] stood looking up into heaven. . . . When the *light* had come forth, Mary worshipped him to whom she saw she had given birth. The child himself, like the sun, shone brightly, beautiful and most delightful to see. . . ."

We see that Jesus is called "the light," that is, something unsubstantial and unfleshy. The midwife goes on: "I, however, stood stupefied and amazed. Fear seized me. I was gazing at the intense bright light which had been born. The light, however, gradually shrank, *imitated* the shape of an infant, then immediately became *outwardly* an infant like a child born normally. I became bold and leaned over and touched him. I lifted him in my hands with great awe, and I was terrified because *he had no weight like other babies*." Jesus outwardly imitated the appearance of a baby, but was not a true baby since he had no weight (how then did the midwife lift him up?), a clearly docetic treatment of the Nativity.

Although docetism faded, one element of this tradition survived and can be seen in many artistic representations of the nativity, namely, Mary's worshiping the child, something that the gospels do not mention.

The apocryphal Infancy Narratives introduced a number of other persons besides Jesus and his parents, for example, Mary's parents Anna and Joachim. In chapter 4 we will see what happened to the Magi, and we have already seen what

Mary worshiping Jesus. Book of Hours (ca. 1500, Rouen workshop). *Arca Artium Collection, Saint John's Abbey and University.*

happened to Zechariah (murdered by Herod). A fourth-century Egyptian bishop named Serapion recounted the last days of Elizabeth and childhood of John the Baptist. Elizabeth died of old age five years after the massacre of the Holy Innocents, the massacre which, the *Protoevangelium of James* tells us, also took the life of her husband Zechariah. Poor John the Baptist was left an orphan. (Ironically, the murderous Herod died on the same day as Elizabeth.)

News of Elizabeth's death caused Jesus to weep. When his mother asked him what was wrong, he told her that her cousin was dead. Suddenly a luminous cloud appeared. Calling for someone named Salome to join them, Jesus and his mother entered the cloud, which took them to the desert place where John was with his mother's body. Mary and Salome washed the corpse and prepared it for burial. Suddenly the angels Michael and Gabriel appeared and dug a grave for Elizabeth. Jesus and Mary stayed with John for seven days of mourning (Salome simply disappeared from the story), and they also taught him how to live in the desert. Mary kindly wanted to take John with them to their home, but her stern son informed her that "this is not the will of my Father who is in the heavens. John shall remain in the wilderness till his showing unto Israel." Jesus tried to placate his mother by promising her that the angel Gabriel would protect John, but Mary continued to weep for the lonely boy and John wept as well when Jesus and his mother got back into the cloud for the return trip to Nazareth.

ACTS OF PILATE

The apocryphal Infancy Narratives also influenced popular accounts of the Passion. From the fifth century came the *Acts of Pilate*, also called the *Gospel of Nicodemus*, best known for its account of Jesus' descent into hell where he freed the souls of the good people of the Old Testament era, a phenomenon the medieval Church entitled the Harrowing of Hell.

In the *Acts of Pilate,* the Roman governor tries to defend Jesus against the accusations of the Jewish leaders who claim that Jesus was born in fornication, that his birth caused the death of the other children, and that his family fled to Egypt because they had lost all respect among their own people. Other Jews defend Jesus and even claim that they had been present at the betrothal of his parents. But Pilate's failure to save Jesus angers the Roman emperor Claudius. Pilate tries to avoid the emperor's wrath by blaming everything on the Jews who wanted the death of a man who had been born of a virgin. But the emperor still sentences him to death. Pilate converts to Christianity just before his death, praying to the Lord, who responds from heaven with the words, "All generations and families of the Gentiles shall call you blessed," a passage from the *Magnificat* (Luke 1:48).

Pilate then dies by decapitation; his wife, here called Procla, "gave up the ghost" and died with him. Oddly enough, this approach has some merit, following the canonical gospel of Matthew in linking Jesus' birth and death, although in a fantastic and unbelievable way.

These early apocryphal stories did much to spread interest in the infancy of Jesus. Most people knew them to be legends, although some parts of them were taken seriously, especially in the Middle Ages. For example, many people believed Anna to be Jesus' maternal grandmother, in spite of her not being mentioned in the gospels and the legendary account of the *Protoevangelium of James* being the only evidence that she ever existed. She eventually became St. Anne.

Far more important was the impact of the stories on Christian art in the Middle Ages and Renaissance, when the stories not only appeared widely but even continued to develop. In an era when people could not read and depended upon visual imagery to understand their faith, the artwork on the doors and walls of churches and cathedrals provided them with the basics of the Bible. Not surprisingly, there were portraits of the creation and the Last Judgment, but also of the life of

Christ, including his birth and many extra-biblical elements, such as the ox and the ass, the three kings, and a gigantic star.

The attitude of the apocryphal writers, that adding to the gospel accounts is acceptable, may seem foreign to us, but even the modern world adds to the nativity story. Gian-Carlo Menotti's 1951 opera "Amahl and the Night Visitors" tells of a crippled Bedouin boy who is cured by the goodness of the magi (now three kings) who stop at his home on their journey to Bethlehem. He joins them on their journey. Also from the 1950s comes the song "The Little Drummer Boy," which tells of a poor young shepherd who wants to bring a gift to the newborn king. Since he cannot bring a gift, he plays his drum for Mary and the infant Jesus, who rewards him with a smile. And let us not forget the convenience-store "art," which rather tastelessly mixes the sacred and commercial by show-ing Santa Claus kneeling beside Jesus' crib. (That manger must have been getting awfully crowded.)

In a little gem, "Court Martial," Charles O'Connor creates the story of one of Herod's soldiers who was sent to kill the boys of Bethlehem (1986), while Jacqueline Wilson has Mary tell the story of Jesus' birth in "Call Me Blessed" (1986). No doubt future creative artists will also add to the story, and why not? It is a great tradition, and the stories have often enriched the feast of Christmas, to which we now turn.

CHAPTER THREE

Creating Christmas Day and the Christmas Season

THE DATE OF CHRISTMAS

By the end of the second century, the Nativity had become part of Christian tradition. With the New Testament canon established, the Infancy Narratives had also become part of the Bible. Yet nowhere in these two centuries do we find any mention of a feast in honor of Christ's birth, that is, no Christmas.

Formidable objections existed to celebrating Christ's birth. The greatest biblical scholar of the period, an Alexandrian named Origen (*ca.* 185–*ca.* 254) pointed out that in the Bible only pagans like Pharaoh or sinful Jews like the Roman puppet king Herod Antipas celebrated their birthdays, and that Herod's celebration had cost John the Baptist his head. Thus Christians should not celebrate the birthday of Christ or of any other biblical figure. But such an objection did not carry as much weight in the third century as it might have in the first. By then the majority of Christians were Gentiles who considered themselves loyal Romans for whom birthday celebrations were merely part of the culture.

Origen's objection represented the personal opinion of a great scholar; a far more difficult *factual* problem presented itself. You cannot celebrate someone's birthday if you do not know on what day she or he was born, and no one knew when Jesus had been born.

As we have seen, no one knew the *year* that Jesus was born. Although many people think the birth occurred at a sort of chronological zero, that is, as the B.C. era passed into the A.D. era, that cannot be. Both gospel accounts say he was born while Herod was king of Judea, and Herod died in 4 B.C. This raises the obvious question of how Christ could be born Before Christ? The answer is quite straightforward. The person who drew up the B.C.–A.D. calendar simply made a mistake.

The first Christians used the Jewish calendar that they knew best. As Christianity moved into the Roman world, and Gentiles more and more made up the Church's membership, the Roman (Julian) calendar replaced the Jewish one. In the fourth century the Roman Empire became Christian, and this would eventually impact the calendar.

About the year 500 a monk named Dionysius Exiguus ("the Little") came to Rome from the Balkans. He was a fine scholar whom the popes employed to edit and organize their documents and archives as well as to translate documents from Greek into Latin because by the sixth century the Latin-speaking and Greek-speaking parts of the Mediterranean world were drifting apart culturally. Eventually the Roman Church asked Dionysius to take on an enduring problem, the tables used to calculate the date of Easter. This got him interested in calendar making in general, and he decided to prepare a new calendar based upon the birth of Christ rather than upon pagan history. For Dionysius history would lead up to the birth (B.C.) and then away from it (A.D., that is, *anno Domini* or "in the year of the Lord"). He relied mostly on the Old Testament and on Jewish, Greek, and Roman historians. According to his calculations, Jesus had been born 754 years after the founding of the city of Rome. But he simply mis-calculated, although no one noticed it at the time.

Later generations of scholars did their own chronological work on both Jewish and Roman history, and they realized that Herod had died in 4 B.C., that is, that Dionysius had erred in calculating Jesus' birth. This corrected dating meant that Jesus could not have been born any later than 4 B.C., and he was possibly born earlier. Matthew tells us that Herod "asked [the Magi] the exact date on which the star had appeared" (2:7) and then later executed all the boys "who were two years old or less, reckoning by the date he had been careful to ask the wise men" (2:16).

As we saw in the first chapter, there are difficulties with the full historicity of Matthew's account, but the evangelist clearly implies that the boy whose birth occasioned the star could have been alive for up to two years while Herod was king. Matthew also speaks of the Flight into Egypt "where [they] stayed until Herod was dead" (2:15), implying at least a stay of some months to which the time of the journey must be added. Biblical scholars thus usually date the Nativity from 4 to 6 B.C.

As for the actual day of the birth, the gospels provide no clue. Luke mentioned that shepherds kept their flocks outdoors on the day of Christ's birth, but shepherds in Judea were outdoors from March until November, a nine-month range that includes spring, summer, and autumn, so not even the season could be determined from the gospels alone.

But could not the date have been passed along by Jesus' mother to his disciples who passed it along to others? (The gospels make no mention of Joseph's being alive during Jesus' ministry, so presumably he had died before then.) Possibly, but this can only be speculation, and if Mary did pass along the date, why did neither Matthew nor Luke record it? Besides, if she was telling them about Jesus' birth, why did she not also tell them more about his life before his public career?

An even greater problem about the date was which calendar were the ancient Christians supposed to use to decipher the date of Jesus' birth? The Jews had a lunar calendar, to which they sometimes added days in order to bring it into harmony with solar calendars, but the match was never precise. The Romans and Egyptians both used solar calendars, but these also did not always match. Yet there were still ways to determine the exact date, although not ways we would find acceptable today.

DATE OF CHRISTMAS AND THE GNOSTICS

The Christian writer Clement of Alexandria (*ca.* 160–*ca.* 220) came from Greece to Alexandria. He recorded that around the year 200 some Gnostic Christians in that Egyptian city had tried to determine the date of Christ's birth.

Most Christians, ancient and modern, followed the Apostle Paul and the four evangelists in believing that Jesus redeemed the world by his suffering and death on the cross. But the Gnostics represented a significant movement among Gentile converts who found that interpretation difficult to accept. In the oldest Greek intellectual tradition, that of the great philosopher Plato, the physical world is but a poor representation of the ideal world beyond our physical senses. This view impacted some ancient Christians. If the physical world were just an inferior creation, how could Jesus redeem us by his physical suffering and death? The Gnostics generally had little regard for the physical world and also for the deity who created it. It would have been better if he had created a world of only spiritual beings.

But if Jesus could not redeem humanity by physical suffering and death, then how could he do it? The Gnostics responded that he brought us knowledge, the knowledge to understand the cosmos and to see through it to the spiritual realities that really counted. The Greek word for knowledge is *gnosis*, which is how these Christians came to be called Gnostics.

Yet if the physical world did not count for much, then why care on what day Jesus was born? For the Gnostics, his birth was not a birth as we understand it, but rather his *manifestation* to humans that he had come from God. Nor did Gnostics agree on the form of his manifestation. Some believed it occurred at his baptism by John in the River Jordan or at the wedding at Cana, his first miracle according to John's gospel. Thus the birth of Jesus interested them only as one possible way he may have manifested himself to the world. But Christians had at least begun to take some interest in his birth. (The Greek word for "manifestation" is *epiphaneia*, from which comes the English word "Epiphany.")

Clement himself did not have a particular interest in the day of Christ's birth, but he does tell us that ". . . there are those who have determined not only the year of our Lord's birth, but also the day; and they say that it took place in the twenty-eighth year of Augustus [= 3 B.C.] and in the twenty-fifth day of the month Pachon." The twenty-fifth day of the Egyptian month Pachon fell on May 20. Clement does not tell us who came up with this date or why, nor did it ever catch on. The same applies to two other dates, the twenty-fourth and twenty-fifth days of the month Pharmuthi, that is, April 19 and 20. Yet the fact that learned Christians in Alexandria were trying to determine the date of Christ's birth proves that they had a real interest in the event. But was their interest purely historical, or did they want to know the date in order to celebrate a feast in relation to it?

In this same passage Clement discussed the views of a prominent Egyptian Gnostic group called the Basilideans, saying that they "hold the day of his [Jesus'] baptism as a festival, spending the night before as a festival" and that some do this on the eleventh day of the month Tubi. In the modern calendar, this date is January sixth, the date of Epiphany for most contemporary Christians and the date of Christmas for some. It was also the date of Christmas for many ancient Christians in the Eastern Mediterranean regions.

For the first time we have a festival associated with a date related to Christmas. But Clement said the Basilidean Gnostics celebrated Christ's baptism on that day, not his birth. This is true, but other factors enter into the discussion.

One is an ancient Jewish tradition that biblical people lived for whole years, a tradition that protected biblical inerrancy. If the Bible said that Moses lived to be 120 (Deut 34:7), then he died at 120 years—not at 119 years and 364 days or 120 years and one day but 120 years of age exactly. Many Christians used this technique and applied it to Jesus. Luke's gospel says that Jesus was "about thirty" (3:23) when he was baptized by John, but generations of Christians have ignored the word "about." It is likely that the Basilideans believed that he had been baptized exactly thirty years after his birth, that is, on January sixth.

Supporting this is the evidence of a fifth-century Balkan Christian named John Cassian, who said that the Egyptians of his day observed the tradition that Jesus had been both born and baptized on that day. So, *if* the Basilideans also celebrated Jesus' birth on January sixth, that date *could* have become acceptable in Egypt—this is probable but not completely proven.

REPLACING PAGAN FEASTS

Yet another factor may have played a role in the promotion of a feast. The ancient Church often promoted a Christian revision of a particular pagan cult or feast. For example, sometime in the late third or early fourth century in the Holy Land, a Christian named George was martyred by the Romans. Local tradition claimed that the mythical Greek hero Perseus had rescued the princess Andromeda in the same locale, and he did so by killing a dragon. As the area became Christian, the local church promoted the cult of George to replace that of Perseus, and in the shifting cultural milieu, St. George acquired his dragon. This approach of reconciling with but not giving in to the existing culture became common. At the end of the sixth century, Pope Gregory I urged the Roman missionaries to Anglo-Saxon England to preserve as much of the local culture as possible while cleansing it of its pagan associations.

JANUARY 6

Other early Christians recorded that the pagan Egyptians observed January 6 as a festival of the virgin-goddess Kore, while still others identified the date as the birthday of the god Osiris. Possibly the Egyptian Christian Gnostics wanted to promote a festival of their own to rival if not supplant existing pagan feasts, and those feasts were birthdays of gods.

But even in the third century the notion that Christ was born on January 6 was encountering opposition, and once again this was because of the complete-years theory. To say that Jesus was exactly thirty when he was baptized on January 6 ignores a rather sizeable problem. The complete-year theory would demand that this date also mark his death, and that was impossible because all the gospels place his death on or about Passover, which falls in the Spring.

Several Christian scholars in North Africa began to disagree with the Egyptians, suggesting an alternate day for Jesus' death—and thus his birth—not just because it was historically feasible but also because it carried symbolic significance. The date was March 25. Why?

MARCH 25

According to the ancient Roman calendar, the spring equinox fell on March 25. Today the spring equinox, which falls on March 21, has a meteorological significance. In the ancient world it symbolized the rebirth or recreation of the earth, the anniversary of the very day when God said "Let there be light." A Roman writer named Hippolytus (*ca.* 170–235) calculated March 25 as both the anniversary of the creation and the date of Christ's death, linking his creation with his redemptive death, which effectively caused the sin-laden world to be born again. An African contemporary named Tertullian (*ca.* 160–*ca.* 220) also held that view about Christ's death. Using the whole-year theory and calculating backward, one could point to March 25 for the date of Jesus' birth,

although neither Hippolytus nor Tertullian did so. But someone must have made this calculation, because in the year 243
an anonymous African Christian sought to correct such a
conclusion.

As we shall soon see, symbolism involving the sun played a
great role in the popular understanding of Christ, to whom
was applied the words of the Jewish prophet Malachi about
the sun of righteousness, "For you who revere my name, the
sun of righteousness shall arise with healing in its wings"
(Mal 4:2). The anonymous African author of a book called
On Computing the Date of Easter contended, following this
symbolism, that the birthday of Christ should most appropriately fall not on March 25—so obviously some people were
celebrating his birthday on that day—but instead on
March 28, the fourth day of creation. This was the day on
which God created the sun and the moon, the sources of
light. Such argumentation sounds strange in an era when we
can dismiss something as "just a symbol," but in the ancient
world symbolic arguments carried great weight. March 28
became a real possibility for the date of the Nativity.

DECEMBER 25

A rather enigmatic third-century Christian with a truly great
name, Sextus Julius Africanus, also believed that March 25
literally was the day of creation and also the date of the
Incarnation, when the Son of God took on a fleshly body to
redeem the world. But Sextus contended that Jesus became
incarnate *not when he was born but when he was conceived*
because the child's flesh was created at conception, which
occurred at the moment the Angel Gabriel told Mary she
would bear a child. This distinction between Jesus' birth and
conception is crucial because *if Jesus had been conceived on
March 25, he would have been born nine months later on
December 25*, the day the Church eventually chose for
Christmas. This approach goes contrary to the common
notion that the feast of the Annunciation was determined by

taking the date of Christmas and going back nine months. In fact, initially the process was just the reverse.

Although a brilliant man, Julius Africanus did not carry much weight in the Christian community. He had served as a soldier under a Roman emperor who had persecuted Christians, and he had later worked as a librarian for a weak and inefficient pagan emperor. These associations may have compromised his influence. But his idea took on more prominence in the fourth century when a variety of other factors pushed the Christians to accept December 25 as the date of Christ's birth. Before we go on to see what those factors were, we should note that none of these third-century writers who tried to calculate the date of Christ's birth made any mention of a festival associated with it, except, perhaps, the Egyptian Gnostics.

SYMBOLIC DATING

The attempt to ascertain the exact date of Christ's birth was just one way the ancient Christians tried to determine the date of Christmas. The other was to adopt some symbols and images common to many religions. This may sound a bit shocking to modern believers, but in fact there are many basic traits that different religions share, such as sacred times (Lent, Hanukah, Ramadan) or ritual meals. The ancient Christians would use such images if they did not contradict the Faith and could help others to understand it. For example, in the Acts of the Apostles, the Apostle Paul refers to the cross of Christ as a Tree, thus portraying wood that symbolized death as wood that symbolized life, while in the gospels Jesus himself uses the image of bread and of living water. As we shall see in the next chapter, one first-century writer compared Christ to the mythical bird, the phoenix. Some of these images and symbols influenced the search for a date for Christmas.

Although the New Testament never calls Christ the Sun, sun imagery is plentiful. Matthew says that at the Transfiguration Christ's face shone like the sun. When Jesus died, this evangelist says that darkness came over the land as the sun disappeared with his death. Mark tells us that the women went to the tomb on the day of the Resurrection as the sun was rising. The Apocalypse tells us that the face of the "one like the Son of Man . . . was like the sun shining with all its force." Possibly the most famous image mentions not the sun specifically but the light in general. In the prologue to John's gospel, the evangelist identifies the Word of God as light, telling us that "the Light shines in the darkness," and he makes it clear that this light was heavenly as was the sun.

The New Testament practice of discerning prophecies of Christ in the Old Testament continued into the early Church. As mentioned earlier, the image in the prophetic book of Malachi, "the sun of righteousness," commanded much attention. It appears in the works of third-century writers such as Clement of Alexandria, Origen, Hippolytus, and the anonymous African Christian who wrote *On Computing the Date of Easter*. It also appears in the writings of the fourth century such as the poet Ephraem and the theologians Athanasius of Alexandria, Ambrose of Milan, and Augustine. To be sure, these writers referred to Christ under a variety of titles, but the prominence of "sun of righteousness" is un-questioned. (If the phrase sounds familiar, that is because it appears in the third stanza of the popular Christmas carol "Hark the Herald Angels Sing," which reads "Hail the Heaven-born Prince of Peace! Hail the Sun of Righteousness!")

But the Christians were not the only ancient people taken by sun symbolism. Many pagans stressed the actual worship of the sun, as in ancient Egypt, and worship of the Sun (*Sol* in Latin) existed in a minor way in ancient Rome as well. By the third century the cult of the Sun had taken a particular turn. In 218 the vagaries of imperial politics had brought to the throne Elagabalus, a teenager who had been a pagan priest in Syria. The new emperor had a great veneration for the Sun and introduced the cult into Rome under the title *deus Sol invictus*, that is, the invincible or unconquered Sun god. Un-fortunately, with sun worship he also included a frenzied cult and even human sacrifice. All this was too much for the staid Romans, who murdered the young emperor in 222. But the cult of the Sun survived the teenage emperor and grew throughout the third century. One of its devotees was another emperor named Aurelian.

The emperor Aurelian ruled from 270 to 275. He feared that the empire was falling apart and needed a source of unity, such as a common religion. Recognizing that fewer and fewer people venerated the traditional gods, such as Jupiter and Venus, he hoped that monotheism might be the answer. Monotheism might also halt the challenge of a growing religion that he thought threatened the empire: Christianity.

In 274 Aurelian instituted the cult of *Sol Invictus*, the Unconquered Sun. He built temples to the Sun, founded priesthoods, and tried to establish a solar theology. But he soon realized that his efforts would not stop Christianity, and in 275 he began to plan a persecution of the Christians, who were saved by the emperor's assassination. Yet Aurelian may still have had an important impact on Christianity, especially since the cult of the Sun did not die with him. The first Christian emperor, Constantine I (306–337), was a devotee of the Sun before his conversion.

To backtrack a bit, the reach of the Romans into Syria also brought the empire into contact with the neighboring kingdom of Persia, from where a virility god named Mithra soon gained favor with Roman soldiers. Mithra, claimed by his devotees to be either the son or companion of the sun, had been born in a cave, and had sacrificed a bull. From this bull emerged the whole of creation, and many images of Mithra show him slaying the bull. At the end of his life, Mithra participated in a feast with the sun, after which he was taken up to heaven in a fiery chariot, as his followers hoped they would be too. Mithra also shared his birthday with the sun god. That day was December 25.

Why would that day be the birthday of the sun god? According to the Roman calendar, the winter solstice fell on that day

(December 21 today). As the shortest day of the year, it signaled the coming continual expansion of daylight. For pagans, it signaled the continual growth of the sun which (or as they would have said, "who") became larger and more powerful day by day. Consequently, they considered the winter solstice to be the birthday of the Sun. Aurelian made December 25, the winter solstice, the birthday of *Sol Invictus* and thus a major feast day throughout the Roman Empire. And here is where one of the most puzzling aspects of establishing the date of Christmas begins.

Many scholars find it virtually impossible to believe that no link exists between the birthday of the Unconquered Sun and that of the Sun of Righteousness (*Sol Iustitiae* in Latin). In 336 the local church at Rome proclaimed December 25 as the *dies natalis Christi*, "the natal day of Christ," that is, his birthday. The document which says this does not justify or explain it. It merely says that this is the day, that is, the date had been accepted by the Roman church some time before and since everyone knew about it, discussion of the date was not necessary. But how long before 336 was the date for Christmas accepted?

Historians have wondered whether the Christians in the late third century had waged a propaganda war against Aurelian, promoting their Sun of Righteousness, the *Sol Iustitiae* against his Unconquered Sun, the *Sol Invictus*. If a propaganda battle between the two Suns indeed occurred, this means that the third-century Christians, especially in the imperial capital, would be stressing the Sun-related aspects of Christ and probably recommending the celebration of his birthday on that of the Sun. We should also recall that several third-century Christian writers had already proposed December 25 as the date of Christ's birth. Aurelian's opponents may have plausibly reasoned that if the date already existed, why not use it against the imperial cult of the Sun?

Does any evidence survive to support this theory? None exists in the formal sense provided by a signed, dated docu-

ment saying, "We chose December 25 as the day of Christ's
Nativity in order to combat the cult of the Unconquered Sun,"
but there are two pieces of evidence that support the theory.

Leo the Great

During his long tenure as pope (440–461), Leo I, known as
the Great, gave a number of Christmas sermons. In sermon
number 7 he says,

> When the sun rises at daybreak, there are some people so foolish
> as to worship it from the highest elevations; even some Chris-
> tians think they are acting piously by following this practice, so
> that before entering the basilica of St. Peter the apostle, dedicated
> to the only living and true God, when they have gone up the
> steps leading to the porch at the main entrance, they turn
> around to face the rising sun and, inclining their heads, bow in
> honor of the brilliant disk.

The seriousness of the problem appears in a less striking but
still important way in Leo's second nativity sermon: "Simple
minds are deceived by some who hold the pernicious belief
that our celebration today seems to derive its high position,
not from the birth of Christ, but from, as they say, the rising
of the 'new sun.'"

Imagine a Christian entering the basilica on Christmas
morning and bowing to the sun! And this in the fifth century
when Christianity had become well-established and was even
the official religion of the Roman Empire.

Neither sermon mentions the Sun of Righteousness, but
both passages clearly show the survival of non-Christian attitudes toward the Sun. Something had fixed the identification
of Christ's birth with the birthday of the physical sun. Might
this be a relic of a third-century propaganda war? It cannot be
proven directly, but it is otherwise difficult to understand why
Christians would be venerating the Sun on Christmas Day as
late as the fifth century. Certainly such practices could not
have arisen *after* the empire had become Christian since the

Christian emperors did their best to weaken and even eliminate paganism.

The second piece of evidence for a third-century propaganda struggle is a work of art, a mosaic on the ceiling of a tomb of the family Julii and now preserved in the necropolis (Greek for "city of the dead") under St. Peter's Basilica in Rome. It portrays Christ driving a chariot through the heavens, just as the pagan sun god Helios did, and Jesus, like the god, has rays of light emanating from his head. The mosaic has no surviving inscription, but Italian archaeologists have named it *Christo Sole*, Italian for "Christ the Sun." They date the mosaic to the late third century, that is, at the time when the emperor Aurelian was promoting the cult of the Unconquered Sun. Significantly, this is the *only* ancient portrayal of Christ as the sun. Historians find it impossible to believe that this portrayal was just coincidentally produced in the city of Rome at the very time when the pagans were promoting the cult of their sun. The Christians must have created this as part of their struggle to turn back the emperor and his Unconquered Sun.

This combination of evidence makes the connection between the birthday of the Sun and the birthday of the Son very likely.

Feast of Saturnalia

One other factor influenced the Roman church to adopt December 25 as the date to celebrate Jesus' birth. Every December the Romans celebrated the feast of Saturnalia in honor of an otherwise minor god named Saturnus. The festival usually lasted for seven days, starting on December 17 and finishing on December 23. During this time the social order was overturned as slaves were allowed a temporary liberty to do what they wanted, for example, they got to dine before their masters did. People exchanged presents, and there was a great deal of eating, drinking, playing games, and often lewd behavior. Presiding over all this raucous activity was the

Saturnalicius princeps, the "Saturnalian prince." Almost all of these practices would reappear in medieval or Renaissance Christmas celebrations, and some survive even today. (On Christmas Day in the British army the officers serve

Christ Driving the Chariot of the Sun. Tomb of the Julii (third century). *Grotte Vaticane, Rome.*

meals to the enlisted men.) But early Christian leaders found the Saturnalian practices offensive.

Since the festival of Saturnalia ended at the latest on December 23, it could not formally determine the date of Christmas. On the other hand, its proximity to the increasingly accepted day for Christ's birth may have led Christian leaders to want to settle the date on December 25 as a counter to the pagan festival, promoting prayerful or at least moral behavior, in sharp contrast to pagan license. (Actually these efforts met little success. As late as the eighth century, the English bishop St. Boniface [d. 754] wrote to Pope Zacharias that during a visit to the Eternal City he had been scandalized by the behavior of Roman Christians during their winter festivities. The pope could only sigh and acknowledge that it was difficult to keep Christians from perpetuating the Saturnalian rituals, although he promised to try to put a stop to it.)

As we saw earlier, the Roman Christians did not tell us why they finally chose December 25 to celebrate the *dies natalis Christi*, but it was not because they believed it to be the exact date of Jesus' birth. While no one piece of evidence finalizes the case, most likely the cult of the Unconquered Sun and the Christian struggle against it along with the tradition of identifying Christ with the prophet Malachi's "sun of righteousness" and the dating of Christ's birth to the day that was also the winter solstice all united in Rome to make December 25 an appropriate if not a chronologically certain date for Christ's birth. When this was combined with the proximity of Saturnalia, the Roman Christians chose a date which had already achieved some acceptance and which could counter two major pagan feasts.

Chronograph of 354

The document containing the affirmation of December 25 as the *dies natalis Christi* in 336 is called the *Chronograph of 354*. The word "chronograph" means "a book which measures time"; in other words, this is a calendar, but a miscellaneous one that includes Easter tables, a list of Roman bishops, and a list of martyrs among other things. A liturgical calendar of martyrs' feasts begins with this reference: "Christ is born on the eighth of the Kalends of January (= December 25) in Bethlehem of Judea." This inclusion may seem odd for a calendar of martyrs' feasts, but Christians considered the dates of death to be their birthdays into heaven, and thus the birthday of Christ made a fitting beginning for such a list. We have arrived at the feast commemorating the birth of Christ on December 25. In other words, we finally have Christmas.

Because of its antiquity and its presence in the capital of the now Christian empire, the Roman church often influenced other churches, although in varying degrees. The churches in the western, mostly Latin-speaking part of the empire generally followed Rome. The churches in the eastern, mostly Greek-speaking areas followed their own traditions, although they maintained regular and fraternal contact with Rome. Most Eastern churches celebrated the feast on January 6 in its Epiphany form and were hesitant about the Roman dating, but many of the Christians who favored the "Sun of Righteousness" title or who had argued for a December 25 feast day were from the East. By 379 the church at Constantinople had accepted the new date, and in 386 the church at Antioch did likewise. The Egyptian church, original home of January 6 as the date of the Nativity, held out longer, but in 431 Alexandria accepted December 25, and the other Egyptian churches followed.

The oldest Christian church, Jerusalem, stuck to a January 6 date until the sixth century. Actually a fifth-century bishop had introduced the new date, but the church reverted after his death, fully accepting December 25 only a century later. Some few Eastern churches retained the old date.

JANUARY 6

But a problem remained. January 6 enjoyed both popularity and tradition, and most Christians wanted to keep it somehow.

The date had originally taken the form of the Epiphany, the manifestation of Christ, first understood as his baptism. In the fourth century a Syrian poet named Ephraem (*ca.* 306– 373) suggested a new interpretation of Jesus' Epiphany, and that was the arrival of the Magi, here symbolizing all the peoples of the world. This view was also gaining prominence in the West at the same time. By the middle of the fourth century the modes of Jesus' manifestation included his birth, the coming of the Magi, his baptism, the wedding at Cana, and the feeding of the five thousand.

The acceptance of December 25 as Christmas eliminated the birth as a possible feast for January 6, but a feast to commemorate the coming of the Magi gained in popularity over the other manifestations because it allowed the Eastern churches to continue to associate January 6 with gospel Infancy Narratives and thus with the Nativity. It also gave a firm meaning to the Epiphany in the Western churches. To be sure, the other meanings for Epiphany did not disappear immediately, but slowly the Magi claimed January 6 as their own day. By the early Middle Ages both December 25 and January 6 had become traditional feast days, except in a few Eastern regions.

We have gone from the year, more or less, of Christ's birth to the day, and now we can speculate on the hour. We do not, of course, mean the chronological hour, which is unknowable from a historical point of view, but the appropriately symbolic hour. The gospels provide no evidence, except that Jesus was born at night, but the Jewish book entitled the Wisdom of Solomon has two verses (18:14-15) which the early Christians applied to Christ's birth: "For while gentle silence enveloped all things, and night in its swift course was now half gone, your [God's] all-powerful word leapt from heaven." Many Early Christians interpreted the phrase ". . . the night half gone . . ." as midnight, and God's Word was Christ.

This interpretation had great appeal in that era because until Christians knew that Dionysius Exiguus had made a mistake in calculating the year of Christ's birth, it seemed miraculously fitting that Jesus was born *exactly at the minute* when the B.C. era was ending and the A.D. era was beginning. This notion of birth at midnight also fostered a sizeable folk-lore such as the belief that animals could speak at midnight on Christmas Eve or that they knelt down at midnight in reverence to the Christ child, but these folkloric interpreta-tions of midnight arose centuries after the early Christian period. The birth at midnight also gave rise to the tradition of Midnight Mass, an essential element of the Christmas liturgical season.

THE CHRISTMAS LITURGICAL SEASON

Our information about the Christmas liturgy derives from two sources, books called Sacramentaries, which include the order of worship and many prayers, and Lectionaries, which included liturgical readings. These books were prepared by religious communities and rarely carry the name of one or two specific authors. Not surprisingly, the more important churches (Jerusalem, Rome, Constantinople) had the greatest but not exclusive influence on liturgical practices.

When Christmas had become accepted as a feast at Rome in the mid-fourth century, the official Christmas Mass was the first one in the morning, usually said around nine o'clock. But the Christians at Jerusalem celebrated a Mass during the night of January 6 in a church built over the cave in Bethlehem that was believed to be birthplace of Christ. (Recall that the Jerusalem church celebrated the Nativity on January 6 in the fourth century.) Thanks to Western pilgrims to the Holy Land, the Latin-speaking churches began to learn of the Jeru-salem practice. In the mid-fifth century the church at Rome followed the lead of Jerusalem and added to Christmas a Mass at midnight, not in St. Peter's Basilica but in the new church of St. Mary Major. This midnight Mass took place in a subterranean chapel that symbolized the cave at Jerusalem.

More than just imitating a Jerusalem custom influenced this decision. As we have just seen, midnight was thought to have been the time when Jesus was born.

The Masses of Christmas

The Roman use of midnight Mass spread to the other Western churches. This midnight service soon came to symbolize the beginning of Christmas Day. Since the Mass meant that Christ had been born, by the eleventh century in England it was called "Christ's Mass," from which comes the word "Christmas."

In the sixth century, after Germanic barbarians had destroyed the Western Roman Empire, the Byzantines, the Eastern Mediterranean successors of Rome, invaded Italy to reestablish imperial rule. They succeeded in taking Rome from the barbarians, and a sizeable group of government officials came from Constantinople to reside in the old imperial city. Many Byzantines venerated St. Anastasia, whose feast day fell on December 25. As a courtesy to the Byzantine community, the pope said a Mass for them at dawn, that is, between midnight Mass and the regular morning Mass. The Mass, however, did not honor St. Anastasia but had the Nativity as its theme. This third Mass, called the *Aurora,* the Latin word for dawn, became part of the Roman liturgical tradition for Christmas, and it was kept after the Byzantines had left Rome. Thus, by the sixth century the Roman church and most other Western churches had evolved a tripartite celebration of Christmas— masses at midnight, at dawn, and in the morning on December 25.

This tripartite celebration also determined the gospel readings for Christmas Day. At midnight the readings were from Luke's account of the census, the Holy Family's journey to Bethlehem, and Jesus' birth, and passages from Isaiah about how "the people who walked in darkness have seen a great light," appropriate for midnight, which was popularly believed to be the darkest time of the night. The second Mass at dawn used Luke's story of the shepherds, commemorating the first people beside Mary and Joseph to recognize Jesus; this Mass also used passages from the Psalms about light, for example, Psalm 97:11, "Light dawns for the righteous." The third Mass used the prologue to John's Gospel which does not recount the Nativity but rather tells of the Word of God becoming flesh. This stressed the divine mystery of the Incarnation and includes the famous reference to the Word of God being the true light which shines in the darkness to enlighten everyone. The light-darkness dichotomy that motivated the "Sun of Righteousness" interpretation of Christ had made its way firmly into the Christmas liturgy.

As Christmas grew rapidly in popularity, its status as a feast began to match that of other feasts, especially Easter, which in turn meant that the Christmas liturgy grew larger and more impressive. For example, many Christians observed vigils on the evening before important feasts, both universal ones such as Pentecost or local ones such as the feasts of martyrs in Roman North Africa. Some ancient Jews practiced vigils, and in Jewish tradition, the day actually begins at sundown. (Genesis pictures God as the creator of this custom because after the creation of light, "there was evening and there was morning, the first day," that is, the very first day ever began in the evening.) By the fifth century a Mass for the Vigil of Christmas in the evening on December 24 was added to the Western liturgies.

Advent

Easter, the feast honoring the resurrection of Jesus, had been a major feast right from the first century, and by the fourth century it had acquired a period of preparation called Lent, which was marked by fasting. Since many people were baptized on Easter Sunday and since baptism was of adults, people fasted in preparation for their baptism. Many scholars believe this pre-baptismal fast formed the basis of the pre-Easter fast, that is, Lent.

This notion of a pre-baptismal fast initiated Advent, although in a round-about way. Into the fifth century in the West, many people were baptized on January 6, which, until it became the feast of the visit of the Magi, had been one of the dates suggested for celebrating Christ's baptism. In the Gallic church (Gaul in Roman times, France later), people began fasting from the feast of the great Gallic saint, Martin of Tours (d. 397), on November 11 to the Epiphany on January 6, a practice known locally as St. Martin's Lent. Since the fasting was relaxed for Saturday and Sunday, the total number of days for the fast was forty, paralleling Christ's time in the desert. The intent of the fast was to give Epiphany the same acknowledgment as a time of baptism as Easter had. This also meant that Gallic Christians were fasting on the days before Christmas.

But as the Western churches began to raise the status of Christmas over the Epiphany, the pre-Epiphany fast began to wane, partly to solidify the December 25 dating. By the late fifth century the Gallic church had a fast from the feast of St. Martin until Christmas. In the Italian city of Ravenna, some fifth-century liturgical references suggest a period of preparation not for Epiphany but for Christmas. By the sixth century, the Roman church definitely had a time of preparation for Christmas, and it was called Advent, which in Latin means "the coming," referring to Christ's coming not on January 6, the day of baptism in Gaul, but to his coming to the whole world on the day of birth, December 25.

Although the Roman Advent included days of partial fasting, called Ember Days, it had more liturgical than penitential overtones. At the end of the sixth century, Pope Gregory I instituted the practice of having four Sunday Masses in Advent, one on each of the Sundays before Christmas. Gregory's Sacramentary also includes three Ember Days. The now familiar Advent was taking shape. Christmas had matched Easter in having a period of preparation that included some fasting. So strong were the penitential overtones of Advent that the Third Sunday of Advent acquired the name *Gaudete* ("Rejoice") Sunday because the period of waiting and, for some, of fasting was coming to a close.

Before going on, we should note that the penitential character of Advent has disappeared under the pressure of the modern Christmas celebrations, especially in the United States where the Christmas season begins right after a major national holiday, Thanksgiving, and includes weeks of shopping, entertainment, office parties, and private get-togethers. How can one be penitent amid the universal rejoicing? The ancient Roman emphasis on the liturgical rather than the penitential character of Advent has literally saved that season. We cannot party and fast, but we can party and pray. On the other hand, it is sad that so ancient a tradition has fallen by the commercial wayside.

Octave of Christmas

The pagan Romans celebrated a major New Year's feast on January 1, just eight days after Christmas. By the sixth century, churches in Spain and France suggested that Christians fast on the first three days of January to counter the pagan aspects of the feast, but, like the Saturnalia, the pagan New Year's feast showed remarkable resilience and longevity. The Roman church, then much influenced by Byzantine practices (several popes of the era were Greek-speakers from Byzantine lands), decided to include the New Year's feast into a Christian schema by celebrating the feast of the Virgin Mary's birth on January 1. (Like that of her son, Mary's birthday was unknown.) This remained popular in Rome, but did not catch on universally.

Since Luke (2:21) had said that Jesus' parents had him circumcised "after eight days," churches in Spain and France instead began to celebrate the feast of the Circumcision. This tradition was not accepted in Rome until the thirteenth century, but the Roman acceptance caused the Circumcision to be a universal feast. (In 1969 the Vatican reinstituted for

Catholics the Marian feast in place of the Circumcision, thus returning to the ancient tradition but upsetting some people engaged in Jewish-Catholic dialogue because the Circumcision was the only feast that emphasized the Jewishness of Jesus.)

Since the eight-day period of December 25 to January 1 included Christmas and the feast of the Circumcision, this became known as the Octave of Christmas. Deriving from the Jewish eight-day celebration of the feast of Tabernacles (Lev 23:36), the liturgical octave first appeared in Christianity in the fourth century as a way of recognizing the importance of a feast. Easter and Pentecost both had octaves as did the Epiphany in the Eastern Mediterranean churches. By the seventh century important saints' feasts also had octaves, such as that of Peter and Paul; even local saints like the Italian martyrs Lawrence and Agnes merited octaves. Inevitably Christmas acquired an octave; the earliest evidence of this dates to the sixth century.

Several important feasts already fell in this period, such as that of St. Stephen, the protomartyr, on December 26, known from the fourth century, and that of St. John the Apostle on the 27th, also known from the fourth century. In the early sixth century the African church added the feast of the Holy Innocents on December 28, thus introducing into the Octave of Christmas a feast directly associated with the gospel Infancy Narratives. In the Middle Ages, Stephen, John, and the Holy Innocents acquired the name *comites Christi* or "companions of Christ" because like him they suffered and could represent three forms of martyrdom. Stephen represented voluntary martyrdom. Tradition said that John was arrested and tortured by pagans, although they did not execute him. He was, however, willing to die. That meant that his was a voluntary "martyrdom" that did not involve execution, thus making him a good example to the vast majority of Christians who would never have to face actual martyrdom. Too young to make a choice, the Holy Innocents represented those who involuntarily and unknowingly died for Christ. The feasts of some other important saints also fell in this period, such as that of Thomas Becket, the twelfth-century English archbishop of Canterbury, on December 29, but he bore no special relation to the Christmas feast, in spite of his being a martyr.

"Little Christmas" and the Twelve Days

Once January 6 commemorated the visit of the Magi, an integral part of the Christmas story, the Church now had a feast that capped off, however unofficially, the Christmas season. For generations, this feast bore the title of "Little Christmas." Although most family crèches have all the figures in place well before Christmas, many churches will not add the figures of the Magi to the crèche until January 6.

In the sixth century, the French church, which used to use January 6 as the date for baptism (from the ancient Egyptian belief that this was the day of Jesus' own baptism), found a way to preserve the importance of the day by proclaiming the twelve days between Christmas and Epiphany to be both a sacred and a festive period. Thus arose the notion of the Twelve Days of Christmas. The notion spread in the Middle Ages, with many people wanting to treat it as a time off from work as well as a time for often raucous merriment and eating, for example, in the European tradition of the Twelfth Night cake. Today the Twelve Days of Christmas are best known via that annoying carol whose words no one can ever remember besides "a partridge in a pear tree." [Encyclopedia editor Gerry Bowler dismisses a widespread notion about this song: that it is "a secret code by which English Catholics kept their faith alive during the Reformation . . . [this] appears to be just another cyber hoax."]

The Annunciation

The establishment of a Christmas season based on December 25 affected several other feasts. It was simple arithmetic to figure out that Jesus' conception had occurred nine months earlier on March 25, and that became the date of the Annunciation (the third-century reckoning of the date of Christmas from the date of the Annunciation had long been forgotten). The feast of the Annunciation was observed rather early in Byzantium, but it did not become a feast in the Latin churches until the seventh century.

The Old Testament book of Leviticus said that a woman who gave birth to a boy was considered to be unclean for forty days. Since Luke's gospel said that Joseph and Mary went to the Jerusalem Temple for purification, by the fifth century early Christians assumed that this occurred forty days after Jesus' birth. Thus the feast of the Presentation in the Temple fell forty days after December 25, that is, on February 2. Since the celebration of the feast involved the carrying of candles in procession, the feast is often known as Candlemas (the "candle Mass").

Finally, since at the Annunciation, now dated to March 25, the angel Gabriel told Mary that her cousin Elizabeth was six months pregnant, the medieval Church concluded that John the Baptist was born three months later, although for no ascertainable reason the date became June 24 rather than June 25.

By the end of the early Christian period Christmas had become a major feast, rivaling Easter in importance. A century and a half of calculation, both arithmetical and symbolic, had produced a feast day, December 25. Working from that date, the Church produced an entire liturgical season, one that stretches forward four weeks before Christmas and for eight or twelve or forty days, depending on the particular feast involved (Circumcision, Epiphany, Candlemas), after Christmas. The formal liturgical season, from the first Sunday of Advent to the Epiphany, covers from five to six weeks of the liturgical year. And all this for a feast that did not even exist in the first or second centuries.

CHAPTER FOUR

Jesus, Mary, the Magi, and an Obscure Asian Bishop

JESUS

One of the oddest elements in the history of Christmas was that many ancient Christians hesitated to observe the feast because they were not sure that Jesus was completely human, and how could they celebrate the feast of his birth if he were not? Strange as this sounds today, it presented a major problem to the early Church and was only resolved by the emergence of a sound Christology.

Christology is the theology of Christ, that is, how Christians understand who he is and what he does. A feast celebrating Christ's *birth* is based upon what we consider a logical assumption, that Jesus was indeed *born* as a human. But this was not obvious in the ancient Church, as the development of Christology proved.

A standard introduction to ancient Christology and trinitarian theology would be several hundred pages long and have extensive explanations of the Greek and Latin technical terminology. Here we offer a brief sketch with emphasis upon clarity. This sketch is necessary because we really cannot understand the development of Christmas in early Christianity without understanding something about the doctrines.

The gospel Infancy Narratives clearly assume that Jesus was born a human being, although conceived in a special way. No New Testament writer doubted his full humanity, although the Epistle to the Hebrews made the vital point that he never sinned. That did not make him less human because ancient Jews and Christians believed sin was a defect in our humanity and not an essential ingredient of it.

Yet the Christians' belief in Christ's humanity was problematic because they also believed that he was divine. This belief appears in the opening chapter of John's gospel where the *Son of God* or "Word" of God is said to be divine, and further along in that gospel Doubting Thomas recognizes Jesus as "My Lord and *My God*." We also have a pagan witness to this belief. In the early second century, Pliny the Younger, a Roman governor in Asia Minor who persecuted Christians, reported to the emperor that the Christians sang hymns to Christ *as a god*.

The problem that arose was: how could Christ be both divine and human, since the two are so distinct? Humans are fallible in every way, God is perfect in every way. Humans are weak, God is omnipotent. Humans are ignorant, God is omniscient. Humans are limited in space and time, God is omnipresent and eternal. Was Christ partly divine and partly human? Is that even possible? But if he was fully human, how could he be at all divine, and if he was fully divine, how could he be at all human? This question provides a good insight into the nature of theology.

That Christ was both human and divine had become a matter of Christian belief. The problem was how to explain that belief, and that is what theology does. Theology is faith seeking understanding; that is, the theologian starts from her or his personal faith and tries to understand and explain it as well as the faith of the community. Early Christian theologians who accepted Christ's humanity and divinity sought a way to reconcile the two.

Ironically, much of the discussion about this was pushed forward by explanations that the larger body of Christians later rejected; some were even labeled heretical. But these explanations emerged when the doctrinal questions involved were still open. Recall that when the Apostle Paul argued that Christianity should go to the Gentiles as well as the Jews, most Christians, who were also mostly Jewish, disagreed with him and probably thought him to be a heretical troublemaker. Only later did they come to believe that Paul carried out the will of the Holy Spirit. Therefore, it is best to see some of those ancient theologians labeled as heretics by later generations as sincere Christians striving with difficult questions.

When Christianity moved out of Palestine and into the larger Greco-Roman world, into Syria, Egypt, North Africa, Asia Minor, Greece, and Italy, it encountered and converted people who thought differently from the first Jewish Christians. These differences appeared very early on with the emergence of docetism.

The docetists believed that a divine, spiritual being could not truly take on corruptible human flesh, so they claimed that Jesus did not have a body; he only "seemed" to have one. He was actually a phantom or a spiritual being appearing to be human, a theme which, as we have seen, appears in some apocryphal gospels.

In a way, docetism presents a logical explanation of the divine-human distinction, but as happened too often in this era, apparently simple and clear-cut answers to the problem usually ignored any number of other issues; in this case, it was the redemption. Christians believed that Jesus had redeemed sinful humanity by his suffering, death, and resurrection, all of which he could only do if he had a real body. Furthermore, only by the most imaginative rereading of the gospel accounts could one deny Jesus a physical body, since the gospels speak of his being born, of his eating and drinking, of his weeping and sweating, and of his dying. Docetism provided too unrealistic a view of Jesus. The larger Church rejected it, but the issue of how human Jesus actually was had been raised.

The second-century Gnostics also had problems with Jesus' body, although they accepted its existence. As we saw in the last chapter, the Gnostics believed that the spiritual self was the true self, and the body was a prison from which the true self had to escape. For them Jesus had redeemed sinful humanity not by the suffering and death of his unimportant material body, but by bringing saving knowledge, or *gnosis*, to the world. They further claimed that they had gotten these ideas via secret traditions passed along in Gnostic circles from the times of the Apostles.

But the larger community of Christians met these threats to their faith not only by insisting on the importance of Jesus' body but also by supporting their beliefs by relying upon the Old Testament and other *Christian* Scriptures. A theologian named Irenaeus of Lyons recognized that there were inspired Christian writings that were on a par with the Old Testament. These Christian books would eventually help to form the New Testament canon. Among these new Scriptures, Irenaeus included Matthew and Luke with their Infancy Narratives. Their account of Jesus' birth would help to emphasize the importance of his physical body. This approach represented an important methodological advance because it meant that future theologians would also have to use Scripture to answer theological questions. This approach weakened the Gnostic arguments, although it did not solve the problem of Christ's being both human and divine.

Origen of Alexandria

Origen of Alexandria, an Egyptian theologian, took a novel approach. The problem facing Christians in determining Jesus' identity was how to link the spiritual deity with the material human body without somehow tainting the divine. By uniting with a pre-existing soul which would animate his human body, the Son of God linked the spiritual existence of the divine and the material existence of the human. Since most Christians did not believe in the pre-existence of souls, Origen's theory also faltered, but most Christians accepted the human soul as the link between the Son of God and the flesh. Jesus was human via his body and soul, and he was divine via the link of his body with a spiritual soul. This meant he could be divine and still have a body, thus making possible a feast for his birth. But this question still had a long way to go before receiving its final resolution.

By the third century theologians had realized that they really could not explain how the Son of God could be both divine and human unless they had explained how belief in the Trinity did not mean polytheism, a belief in three gods. A North African theologian named Tertullian worked out a trinitarian theology by suggesting that the Trinity consisted of three individual persons who shared the same substance. But he did not think all persons in the Trinity were equal; he believed the Son was subordinate to the Father, a very common view in the third century.

Council of Nicea

The Trinitarian problem returned with finality in the early fourth century. In 321 an Egyptian priest named Arius took the widespread view that the Son was subordinate to the Father to its logical conclusion. He argued that if the Son were less than the Father, then he could not be really divine. How can a divine being ever be *less* than any other being? Arius therefore concluded that the Son was a creature—a perfect creature and superior to humans in ways we could not even imagine, but a created being none the less. There was a time when the Son did not exist, and the Father had created him. These views went against the common Christian belief, and most Egyptian bishops severely rejected Arius' views. But Arius proved a difficult man to refute. To the surprise of the Egyptians, several bishops in Palestine supported him. The

resulting conflict threw the churches of the eastern Mediterranean into turmoil.

But a new force had entered Christian life. The Roman
emperor Constantine had become a Christian by 321, and he
hoped that his new religion would help to unite the empire.
Appalled at the divisions in the eastern churches, he came up
with a new idea: a council of all the bishops in the world to
discuss and settle the Arian question. The Greek word for the
inhabited world was *oikuméne*, and this council became
known as the first ecumenical council. It met in 325 in the
city of Nicea in northwest Asia minor, just across the water
from the new capital of Constantinople, literally, "the city of
Constantine." (The first Christian emperor occasionally
indulged in the sin of pride.)

The bishops at Nicea dismissed the teaching of Arius and
expounded their own trinitarian theology. They said that
Father and Son were divine, equal, and independent, but they
were united by sharing the same divine substance, much as
humans share the substance called humanity. After the
council, some churches substituted "essence" or "being" for
"substance," for example, many Christians today say that the
Son is "one in being" with the Father. This formulation was a
controversial step to take. Conservative critics complained
that none of this could be specifically found in Scripture, but
the bishops at Nicea needed some way to answer Arius and
explain what the Trinity was. They were doing theology.
Furthermore, although their formulation could not be found
expressly in Scripture, neither did it contradict Scripture.
Acceptance of this approach freed Christian theologians to
interpret the Bible by using language from other spheres
(much the way modern biblical exegetes use social science
and literary tools). Oddly enough, although the bishops at
Nicea responded to Arius' views on the Son, they passed up
the chance to affirm the full divinity of the Holy Spirit. That
was accomplished by bishops at a second ecumenical council
in Constantinople in 381.

Now that the Christians had established who the Son of God was in relation to the Trinity, they could finally turn to establishing how this divine Son became human.

Apollinaris vs. Gregory

Late in the fourth century a bishop in Asia Minor named Apollinaris taught that the Son of God united with the flesh of Christ, but that Christ had no human soul, mind, or will because he did not require them. As a divine being, the Son of God had a mind and a will which were both perfect, so these supplanted the human faculties in Jesus. Furthermore, a divine spiritual being did not need a soul. This approach provided a logical and coherent explanation of the human-divine dilemma, but one that overlooked a serious problem: human salvation.

Apollinaris' opponents, led by another Asian bishop, Gregory of Nazianzen, argued from the theology of salvation. Gregory saw in Apollinaris' teaching echoes of theories that denied Christ's full humanity. How could he be fully human without a human soul, mind, and will? And how, Gregory demanded, could Christ redeem humans if he had not been fully human himself? As Gregory put it, what Christ had not taken on, he could not save; if he did not take a complete human nature to himself, he could not save our complete human natures. The Church agreed with Gregory against Apollinaris. Jesus had to be fully human. But still other questions about Christ's humanity and divinity lay in the future.

Council of Ephesus

In 428 a bishop of Constantinople named Nestorius began preaching against the use of the title "Mother of God" for Jesus' mother Mary, a title which first appeared in the third century and was widely popular among believers. Nestorius opposed it on the grounds that a human could not be the mother of the divine. In so doing, he aroused the enmity of

Cyril, bishop of Alexandria, who feared that denying Mary that title would separate too widely the divine and human in Christ and thus threaten their unity. This unity in the one Christ made the title Mother of God permissible. Regrettably, the theological dispute got caught up in ecclesiastical politics because Constantinople and Alexandria were rivals in the eastern part of the Roman empire. Their dispute was settled in 430 at the third ecumenical council which met in the city of Ephesus. The council approved Cyril's teaching, that the divine and human were so united in the one person of Jesus Christ that Mary, as human mother of that person, could legitimately be venerated as the Mother of God.

The Council of Ephesus did not completely settle matters. In 449 a Constantinopolitan priest named Eutyches taught that there were indeed two natures in Christ, but they existed *before* the Incarnation. Once the divine Son of God united with the human nature, the divine swallowed up the human, leaving only one nature, the divine. The word for "one nature" in Greek is Monophysitism. Many Christians, including the bishop of Constantinople, opposed this new teaching, but politics entered the controversy. Eutyches found support from the new bishop of Alexandria, Dioscorus, who, like Cyril, wished to weaken the rival bishopric of Constantinople. Dioscorus hastily called a council at Ephesus in 449; the council supported Monophysitism.

Council of Chalcedon

Many Eastern bishops as well as Pope Leo I of Rome thought Monophysitism denied Christ's true humanity by abolishing his human nature after the Incarnation, so they called the fourth ecumenical council, which met in the city of Chalcedon in 451. The assembled bishops formulated the Christology accepted by most Christians: Jesus Christ is one person with two natures, one human and one divine, and that these two natures both inhere in him but do not impinge upon each other. Jesus is fully human and fully divine. The Council of

Chalcedon did not explain how Christ can be human and divine since this is ultimately a mystery, but it affirmed the faith of the Church and established a theology to support it. (The council may have settled the doctrinal question, but Monophysitism continued as a religious movement, becoming very popular in the Near East. The contemporary Coptic Christians of Egypt are among the descendants of the Monophysites.)

Future theologians may rethink or rework the Chalcedonian formulation, but the full humanity of Christ was from then on a matter of faith. Christmas had been a major liturgical event for a century before Chalcedon, but after that council, the doctrinal appropriateness of a feast celebrating Christ's birth could no longer be questioned. He had been born as a fully human person.

MARY

Despite the enormous devotion to Mary in many churches over the centuries, she does not appear often in the New Testament. Think of the biblical accounts of Mary: the Annunciation, the Visitation, the birth of Jesus, the visit by the shepherds, the presentation in the Temple, and the finding of the twelve-year-old Jesus in the Temple. All of these events occur in the first two chapters of one gospel, Luke. Matthew adds the flight into Egypt. Mark mentions Mary by name once when the skeptical people of Nazareth say of Jesus, "This is the carpenter, the son of Mary," and then refuse to listen to him. Mary actually appears in only one Markan passage, the one in which Jesus declares that "anyone who does the will of God, that person is my brother and sister and mother," that is, a passage that plays down the importance of physical relationship to Jesus. John's gospel adds two more incidents about her, although that gospel does not ever use the name "Mary," instead referring to her as the mother of Jesus. John tells of the wedding feast at Cana, and he also adds that she was under the cross. Luke includes a non-gospel reference. In the beginning of the Acts of the Apostles, he tells how Mary joined the closest disciples of her son in the upper room after Jesus' resurrection and ascension.

Mary appears nowhere else in the New Testament. The Apostle Paul makes an oblique reference to her in the Epistle to the Galatians when he says that Jesus was born of a woman, but this just affirms his common humanity with us because except for Adam who, Genesis recounts, was created from the earth and Eve who was created from Adam, all humans were born of women. Paul does not mention Mary by name or refer to her by such titles as the mother of Jesus.

The paucity of New Testament references to Mary outside the Infancy Narratives shows another consequence of the rise of Christmas. The feast of Jesus' birth is also the feast of Mary's maternity. To be sure, Jesus is the incomparably more crucial figure, but Mary's significance for the feast cannot be overlooked. As Christmas rose to importance in the Early Church, the role of Mary as the mother of the newborn Savior also became increasingly important. Much of this new status manifested itself in devotion, as we saw with the *Protoevangelium of James*, but it also manifested itself in doctrine, often but not always in relation to the Nativity.

Outside the New Testament, the first theological reference to Mary appears in the works of the second-century writer Justin the Martyr, who compared Mary to Eve, probably drawing from the Apostle Paul's comparison of Adam and Christ in the Epistle to the Romans. The Mary-Eve comparison became the most common theological understanding of Jesus' mother before the fifth century. Another second-century theologian, Irenaeus of Lyons augmented the parallel between Eve and Mary into a comparison of their roles, one being the woman who brought sin into the world and the other being the woman who brought into the world humanity's redeemer from sin. All early theologians pointed to the virginal conception as a miracle which proved the divine origins of Christ.

Actually, the most important female in second-century Christianity was the Church, which appears clearly as a woman for the first time in Rome in the mid-second century in *The Shepherd of Hermas*, a prophetic work by a Jewish Christian. This image caught on quickly, and it took on maternal imagery in the third century when Cyprian, a bishop-martyr in North Africa, portrayed the Church as a woman and imaged the Old and New Testaments as her two breasts by which she nourished the faithful. The Mother of Jesus did not cease to be important, but ecclesial female imagery was stronger. Yet with the growth of interest in the gospel Infancy Narratives in the third century, interest in Mary grew correspondingly. The parallel with Eve continued throughout the early period, but now much emphasis fell upon her virginity as affirmed by the gospel Infancy Narratives. Her virginity before the birth of Christ was a given because of its biblical foundation, but starting in this century writers commonly spoke of her perpetual virginity, which more and more included the physical integrity of her body, unchanged by the birth of her son, a popular belief first evident in the apocryphal Infancy gospels but now being augmented by theology.

With the increasing acceptance of the Christmas feast in the fourth century, the prominence of Mary in Luke's Infancy Narrative increased her prominence in thought and devotion. Virtually all fourth-century writers cited the Mary-Eve comparison, and belief in her perpetual virginity became widespread. Late in the fourth century, a Latin Christian named Helvidius suggested that Mary and Joseph had other children than Jesus, citing the "brothers" of Jesus referred to in the gospels and explained in the apocrypha as sons of Joseph by a previous marriage. When his views became public, several prominent Latin theologians defended Mary's perpetual virginity.

It is also in the fourth century that writers such as the Syriac poet Ephraem and the great theologian Gregory of

Nyssa, commenting on the Nativity, initiated the view that Mary gave birth to Jesus without birth pangs, a crucial point. In Genesis 3:16 God tells Eve (to whom the theologians were comparing Mary), ". . . in pain you shall bring forth children," that is, labor pains in birthing were one of the consequences of original sin. Ephraem and Gregory were saying that Mary had been spared one of the consequences of original sin, but how could that be since she was a descendant of Adam and Eve? These are early indications of what would eventually become the doctrine of the Immaculate Conception, which is the belief that Mary was born free of original sin. The early Church never affirmed this doctrine unequivocally, but more and more theologians supported it, demonstrating the expansion of Marian theology and piety in the period.

The growing belief in the Immaculate Conception soon led to the belief in the bodily assumption of Mary into heaven. How could she be free from just one of the consequences of original sin? Logically she would have to be free from all of them, including death. By the fifth century the Syrian church had produced an apocryphal gospel, the *Transitus Beatae Mariae*, literally "the passing over of Blessed Mary," which spoke openly of Mary's bodily assumption into heaven, thus sparing her body the decay to which all others were subject. In the Middle Ages the Immaculate Conception and Assumption grew in popularity and theological acceptance. The Roman Catholic Church defined as dogma the Immaculate Conception in 1854 and the Assumption in 1950. The sixteenth-century Protestant Reformers did not accept these as dogmas, nor do modern Protestants.

As our discussion of Jesus just showed, the most crucial Mariological issue facing the early Church was whether Mary could be called the "Mother of God," an issue settled at the ecumenical Council of Ephesus in 430 which affirmed that the one person of Christ united both the human and divine, and since Mary was the mother of that person, she could reasonably bear the title Mother of God. At first glance, this definition may seem a long way from the gospel accounts, but Mary could not have been understood as the Mother of God had the biblical Infancy Narratives not affirmed her as the Mother of the human Christ.

Both Marian theology and devotion experienced significant growth throughout the history of the Church, especially, of course, in Catholic circles. This growth had its base not just in the gospel Infancy Narratives but also in the importance that the feast of Christmas had given to Mary in the early Church.

THE MAGI

Matthew's gospel (2:1-12) reports that magi "from the East" came to pay homage to Jesus and to offer him gifts of gold, frankincense, and myrrh. He does not mention how many of them there were, where they traveled from or what mode of transportation they used. He does not call them kings, give them names, or describe them. Tradition filled in the details.

The Magi enjoyed enormous popularity in early Christianity for two reasons. First, they were Gentiles. Jesus, his parents, his relatives (the family of John the Baptist), the shepherds, and the Temple prophets, Simeon and Anna, were all Jewish. As the Church became increasingly Gentile, the new converts understandably took a great interest in the only non-Jews to play a role in the Infancy Narratives.

The second reason is that the Magi were mysterious and almost romantic. Unnamed, unnumbered, they came "from the East," following a star, and they just as mysteriously disappeared, warned in a dream to return home a different way. These pagan astrologers traveled a long way to venerate to the newborn king of the Jews, a remarkable sign of devotion, and Matthew so well contrasts the believing, committed magi to the devious and ruthless Herod. If ever biblical figures were ripe for speculation, the Magi were the ones.

Since the Early Christians believed that Jesus had fulfilled the prophecies of the Old Testament, they looked there first for details about the Magi. As we saw in chapter 2, the only specific reference in Matthew's account is to the gifts, and the prophet Isaiah spoke of "nations" acknowledging the Lord by coming from afar bearing gold and frankincense. Those who come to the Lord will travel by camels, so the Early Christians gave the magi a mode of transportation.

But the book of Isaiah hinted at even more. Isaiah 60:3 said that "nations shall come to your light, and kings to the brightness of your dawn." To this the early Christians added Psalm 72:10, a passage traditionally used in the Epiphany liturgy, "May the kings of Tarshish and of the isles render him tribute, may the kings of Sheba and Seba bring him gifts." No gospel passage spoke of foreign kings coming to visit Jesus and bringing gifts. The Magi were the only foreigners to pay him homage, and they did bring gifts. Soon Christian theologians applied these Old Testament verses to the Magi. Around the year 200 the African theologian Tertullian observed that ". . . the East generally regarded the magi as kings," and he next connected them with Christ as the recipient of riches of the East. The view that they were kings was taken up in the fourth century by the Syrian poet Ephraem. The notion of their kingship did not catch on very quickly in the Western part of the Roman Empire, but around 500 a Gallic bishop named Caesarius of Arles stated clearly that they were kings. In the Middle Ages their royal stature was simply taken for granted, as it has been ever since.

But by following out the expansion of the biblical reference in making the Magi into kings, we have jumped ahead chronologically. Let us now go back to the first and second centuries to see how the many traditions about the Magi originated, developed, and coalesced.

At the end of the first century, a writer named Clement of Rome tried to show natural parallels to the resurrection. He cited a remarkable bird called the phoenix. There is only one of its kind, it lives for five hundred years, and then it consumes itself in a fire, but from that fire emerges a new phoenix. Today we would hardly consider that an adequate parallel to the Resurrection, but many people in the ancient world believed the phoenix to be real. Clement said that this bird lived in Arabia and built its nest of frankincense and myrrh, thus identifying Arabia as the home of these two spices. Although he did not connect this with the Magi, later writers would.

In the early second century a Syrian bishop named Ignatius of Antioch traveled under guard to Rome where he was thrown to the beasts in the arena. On his journey he wrote letters to several churches. In his letter to the church at Ephesus, he recounted some marvelous elements in the life of Christ. One of these was the appearance of a star at the time of his birth. "A star blazed forth in the sky, outshining all the other stars, and its light was indescribable, and its novelty provoked wonderment, and all the starry orbs, with the sun and the moon, formed a choir around that star; but its light exceeded all the rest, and there was perplexity as to the cause of its unparalleled novelty."

The exceptional brightness of the star also appears in the apocrypha, but Ignatius has added the detail that its appearance produced "wonderment " among people. He also used the image of the other stars forming a chorus about the new star, probably symbolizing Christ as the star and the rest of creation as the other stars. This would fit a primary Christian theme, that the natural world recognized Christ—recall the portents at his death in Matthew's gospel and the apocryphal accounts of animals accompanying the Holy Family in Egypt and the palm tree bending over at the baby Jesus' command.

Ignatius addressed another issue. Ancient magi had varying reputations. Some received honors as priests and scientists (astrology was a science in those times), while others were scorned as charlatans and magicians. Charlatans were simply crooks, but magicians were believed to call upon divine or demonic powers, and that made them rivals to other religions, including Christianity. In the Acts of the Apostles, Peter has a run-in with a magician named Simon, who is actually referred to as Simon *Magus* (Latin for *magos*) in Christian tradition. A second-century apocryphal work, the *Acts of Peter*, continues their rivalry in Rome. So for many early Christians, recognition of the infant Christ by the Magi was not necessarily a good thing. But Ignatius refutes that. "This [the appearance of the star] was the reason why every form of magic began to be destroyed, every malignant spell to be broken, ignorance to be dethroned, an ancient empire [the reign of Satan] to be destroyed. . . ." The veneration of the Savior by good magi heralded the destruction of the entire corrupt world of which the evil magi were a part.

Another second-century author, Irenaeus of Lyons, provided an interpretation of the gifts: ". . . myrrh because it was for him who should die and be buried for the mortal human race; gold because he was a king 'whose kingdom has no end'; and frankincense because he was God. . . ." He correctly interpreted Matthew's gospel by linking Jesus' birth with death. By interpreting the gifts symbolically, Irenaeus also started a tradition that played a large role in the Middle Ages. The gifts came to symbolize any number of worthwhile things, such as the three theological virtues (faith, hope, and charity), the three parts of the world (Africa, Asia, Europe), and the three parts of philosophy (logic, physics, ethics).

The third century brought more additions to the magi tradition. As we just saw, the North African writer Tertullian asserted that they were considered kings in the East. He added another detail, here following Clement of Rome. The "East" meant Arabia for Tertullian because that land provided the kind of spices that the Magi had brought.

But Clement of Alexandria disagreed. He knew a great deal about the Near East, and he believed that the Magi came from Persia. In that kingdom the Magi functioned as priests of Zoroastrianism, a somewhat fatalistic religion founded in the sixth century B.C. by an obscure figure named Zoroaster. The Persian magi enjoyed great reputations as astrologers, which is not surprising since astrology is a form of fatalism, asserting that the stars determine much of our lives. Clement spoke of "the Magi of the Persians who foretold the Savior's birth and who came into the land of Judea, guided by a star." But Clement had more to add. Citing a supposed saying of the Apostle Paul which is not in the New Testament, Clement said that Paul quoted a visionary Persian book which prophesied the coming of Christ. Support for Clement's view came from the apocryphal *Arabic Infancy Gospel*, which says that Zoroaster himself predicted the birth of Christ. In general the Alexandrians followed Clement's view that the Magi came from Persia.

The other great third-century Alexandrian, Origen, changed our image of the Magi forever by a comment upon the life of the Hebrew patriarch Isaac. In the book of Genesis God asks Abraham to sacrifice his son Isaac in order to test Abraham's faith. The sacrifice will take place on a hill, and Isaac has to carry the wood for the sacrifice up the hill. Before Abraham kills the boy, an angel intervenes and Isaac is saved. As the only son, the bearer of the promise, and someone who carried the wood for his death up a hill, Isaac was the archetypal symbol of Christ in the early Church, and the story of his sacrifice appears frequently in Christian art.

Origen provided commentary upon an obscure text in the book of Genesis. In chapter 26, Isaac met three men who previously hated him but who recognized that the Lord was with him and so made a covenant with Isaac. Working from the traditional symbolic identification of him with Christ, Origen interpreted the three men, pagans who sought reconciliation with Isaac, as symbols of the Magi, who "came from Eastern regions," having learned from their sacred books and the traditions of their elders about the birth of Christ. In claiming that the Magi knew of Christ from their sacred books, Origen followed his teacher Clement, but he broke new ground by claiming that *three* men symbolized the Magi. Ever since then, Christians have accepted that there were three Magi.

Why did Origen think there were three of them? He did not say, but it is most likely that he got the number from the three gifts. Yet it is a bit incongruous that this interpretation, which changed forever how Christians picture the Magi, occurred not in a scholarly analysis of the Gospel of Matthew but in a homily written on an obscure passage in Genesis.

In the sixth century the Syrian church began to claim that there were twelve Magi. This may have resulted from popular tales about the Magi returning to their homes and becoming evangelists about Christ, even though they experienced him only as an infant and knew nothing about his subsequent life and death. The number twelve obviously parallels that of those other great ancient evangelists, the Twelve Apostles. Syrian sources say that the "magi evangelized and imposed Christianity only *after* they had been baptized by the apostle Thomas," that is, by a disciple who knew about the adult and risen Christ, the heart of the first apostolic preaching. (According to Eastern tradition, Thomas, one of the Twelve, had evangelized as far east as India.) By the seventh century, the twelve Magi or twelve princes—their royalty had also migrated eastward—had become a staple of Syrian tradition.

In the fourth century the Church established the feasts of Christmas and Epiphany. This guaranteed that the account of the Magi would always have a major place in the Christmas cycle of feasts. Also in that century, individual Christian writers continued to add on details to the story. The Syrian poet Ephraem, who constantly saw travelers "from the East" pass through his country, argued that the Magi must have been Persians, and he described the route which they would have taken from Persia to Bethlehem. The Roman emperor Julian (361–363), known as Julian the Apostate because he had been raised a Christian but abandoned the faith for paganism, claimed that the Persian king sent the Magi as ambassadors, which is why they brought gifts. Much as the Christians understandably loathed Julian, John Chrysostom and Augustine both took up the image of ambassadors, although they allegorized it to make it non-political, for example, interpreting them as ambassadors representing the believing Gentiles in contrast to the unbelieving Jews.

The notion of ambassador appeared someplace else—Christian art. In the fourth century the Magi began to appear in various forms of Christian art, often in decorations on

The three magi and Mary on a throne (fourth century).
Catacomb of Priscilla, Rome.

sarcophagi or carved stone tombs. Since the Roman Empire had become Christian in the fourth century, the art reflected imperial values. The Magi were often shown approaching Jesus and Mary, who is frequently shown seated on a throne(!), as ambassadors bearing gifts to royalty. They are always three in number, and they wear the traditional clothing of either Asia Minor or Persia. (Mary on a throne would be a major feature of medieval art as well. Only in the realistic art of the Renaissance did she again become the humble young woman of the gospels.)

Fourth-century art introduced another element to the story. Representations of the star sometimes show an angel within the star, demonstrating that the star was more than natural and blending this "annunciation" to the Magi with the other annunciations that were given by angels. Some representations show the Greek letters ι (iota) and χ (chi), the first letters in the words Jesus and Christ, printed on the star, or the Chi-Ro, an X on the stem of a P, the first letters in the name Christ. This tells the viewer that, via the star, Jesus himself called the Magi to Bethlehem.

The Magi see the Chi-Ro inside the star. Sarcophagus (fourth century).
Pio Cristiano, Rome.

Other details just kept on coming. The Spanish poet Prudentius (348–ca. 407) wrote that the Magi brought all three gifts in golden containers. In Matthew's gospel, the Magi only speak once, when they ask Herod, "Where is the child who is born king of the Jews? For we observed his star at its rising and have come to do him homage." But the Syrian poet Ephraem created a dialogue between Mary and them. The dialogue is very formal, yet it adds to the traditions about the Magi. In Ephraem's poems, Mary dialogues with the Magi as a group; no *magos* speaks individually. That is understand-able partly because they act only as a group in the gospel and partly because the poet cannot have persons speaking individually unless they have names, and this leads us to the great contribution of the fifth and sixth centuries.

The gospel account provided so little information about the Magi that the early Christians desired more, yet the very paucity of the account allowed the imagination to soar. We have seen that to Matthew's simple account of how "wise men from the East came to Jerusalem" by following a star, biblical allegory and pious creativity had provided the camels, the number of the Magi and their native countries, interpretive meanings for the gifts, royal status, and additional dialogue. They also made the star the largest and brightest star in history and one that contained either the image of an angel or the first letters in the name "Jesus Christ." With the infallibility of hindsight, we can say that it was inevitable that someone would have to give them names.

Names of the Magi

Historian Bruce Metzger tells us, "The earliest literary reference to the names of the Magi occurs in what is generally called the *Excerpta Latina Barbari*. This document . . . is in the form of a chronicle . . . drawn up by an Alexandrian Christian who lived, it seems, in the sixth century. . . ." Translated, the reference from the book reads: "In those days during the reign of Augustus . . . the magi brought him (Jesus) gifts and venerated him. The magi are called Bithisarea, Melchior, and Gaspar." So here, in the earliest extant written work, we have the familiar names (Bithisarea was more popularly spelled Balthasar). But where did these names come from?

The name Balthasar is probably a corrupted form of Belteshazzar, the name given to the Jewish prophet Daniel in the Babylonian court. Melchior may derive from two Hebrew words, *melek* meaning "king" and *or* meaning "light," thus "king of light." He was often thought to be the king who brought the gold, possibly because the brightness of gold recalled the light. Caspar or Gaspar (both forms were widely used) may be a corruption of the name Godaphar, a famous Indian king, who appears in an apocryphal writing called the *Acts of Thomas*, which deals with the adventures of the Apostle Thomas in India (presumably it was on this journey that Thomas baptized the magi). We say that these origins for the names "may be" true because the names are all obviously fictitious, and no ancient author tells us how they originated. The anonymous author of the book that contains the names does not explain or justify them. This suggests that by the sixth century the names had already become common and may date as early as the fifth century.

Whatever the case, the names caught on quickly. In the Latin West, the first written reference to their names is in an obscure, anonymous work, probably from Britain or Ireland, called the *Collectanea*. It may date to the sixth century, and it gives the familiar names Melchior, Balthasar, and Caspar. It describes Melchior as old and the bringer of gold, Caspar as young and the bringer of frankincense, and Balthasar as an African and the bringer of myrrh.

Venerable Bede

Although from the British Isles, the *Collectanea* has an uncertain date, but we have definite dates for the English monk and scholar, the Venerable Bede (673–735), who wrote, "Spiritually interpreted, the three magi signify the three parts of the world, Asia, Africa, and Europe, that is, the entire human race, which took its origins from the three sons of Noah." Bede had gotten this idea from the African theologian Augustine, who claimed that the magi represented the entire Gentile world. Since the medieval Christians knew of only three continents, Bede believed that if the Magi did represent the whole world, then they represented the three continents. His interpretation caught on in the West, and it is the reason why pictorial representations of the Magi often show them as representatives of those continents.

But Bede used more than Augustine as a source. A great biblical scholar, he searched the Old Testament for some fore-shadowing of the Magi. The search did not take long. Realistically, the only biblical book that could speak of the whole world was Genesis, which told of the world in its formation. In Genesis, after the Flood, Noah's family had to repopulate the earth. Since the ancient Israelites knew of only three races of people, Noah had three sons. Shem was the father of the Semitic peoples (the group to which Israel belonged), Ham was the father of the African peoples (the Israelites had been enslaved in Egypt and knew of African peoples), and Japeth was the father of the Indo-European peoples (the invading Philistines were Indo-Europeans). We can see here how an earlier scholar's work on Genesis determined Bede's interpretation. Allegorizing a Genesis passage, Origen had concluded there were three Magi. By the time Bede allegorized another Genesis passage, the three Magi had become an accepted fact, and it never occurred to Bede that there were other than three of them. When he alighted upon the three sons of Noah, he had exact confirmation of his belief that the three Magi represented the entire world, even to the point of knowing what races they represented.

While Bede settled the matter for the Latin West, more variety prevailed in the East. A sixth-century Syrian treatise identifies the Magi as Hormizdad, king of Persia; Yazdegerd, king of Sabha; and Perozadh, king of Sheba (the last two place-names are taken from Psalm 72). In an Armenian apocryphal Infancy Gospel of the High Middle Ages, their names are Melkon, king of Persia; Gaspar, king of India; and Balthasar, king of Arabia, although an alternate tradition has Matathilata, Thesba, and Salahotatha. The Egyptians we have dealt with were Greek-speaking Alexandrians, but the Coptic Christians of rural Egypt called them Bathezora, Melchior, and Thaddias. And what of the Persian Christians, who lived in the supposed homeland of the Magi? They gave the names as Amad, Zud-Amad, and Drust-Amad. And what about the Syrians who believed that the Magi numbered twelve? No problem. They simply invented twelve names, which survive in a tenth-century document: Ahduiyad, Hadundad, Shethaph, Arshik, Zerwand, Arihu, Artahshasht, Eshtanbuzon, Mahdum, Ahshiresh, Sordolah, and Marduk.

In fact, the Syrian Christians had such a fondness for inventing names that they decided to provide names for the shepherds who went to see Jesus. A thirteenth-century work, the *Book of the Bee*, gives their names as Asher, Zebulon, Justus, Nicodemus, Joseph, Barshabba, and Jose.

The Magi in Art

The ancient Jews were aniconic, that is, they did not make representations of people, although there were exceptions among Diasporan Jews. This is why we have no images even of great kings like David or Solomon; it also why none of Jesus' followers made an image of him from life. As the Church became Gentile, more and more Christians wanted to make images, and artists began to produce them in the third century. Since the artists had no existing tradition to work from, they blatantly borrowed from pagan art, using busts of Alexander the Great to model the face of Christ. By the fourth century, Christian art had blossomed, and it included many representations of the Magi. But these were often unimaginative, just showing them as three men in Persian clothing bringing gifts. Occasionally, in large churches like the fifth-century St. Mary Major in Rome, the artists used more imagination, showing the three Magi in rich, elaborate clothing.

The dominant image of the Magi for subsequent centuries came from the Italian Adriatic seaport city of Ravenna, the sixth-century capital of the Byzantine governor in Italy. The church of St. Apollinaris Nuovo, built by Byzantines in the 540s, contains a mosaic of the three Magi with the names Balthassar, Melchior, and Gaspar. This large, beautiful work represents the first definite appearance in the West of the three names of the Magi (although Balthassar would soon lose the second 's'). Furthermore, since the images of the Magi in this mosaic correspond to the descriptions of them given by the anonymous author of the *Collectanea*, the author of the first Western book with their names must have been a British or Irish pilgrim to Italy who had seen the church of St. Apollinaris Nuovo.

This mosaic, portraying the Magi in the elaborate clothing of Persian royal ambassadors, reflects Byzantine imperial art. Mary sits on a throne, holding Jesus on her lap. The Magi do not actually give her the gifts. Rather, an angel stands next to

+SCS BALTHASSAR +SCS MELCHIOR +SCS GASPAR

The Magi portrayed in a mosaic in the Church of St. Apollinare Nuovo (sixth century). *Ravenna, Italy.*

the throne, ready to accept the gifts and show them to Mary. This is how the Byzantine emperor received the offerings of visiting ambassadors, so the suggestion by the fourth-century Roman emperor Julian, that the Magi represented a delegation sent by the Persian king, colored their portrayal in Christian art.

Although this mosaic set the pattern for the ethnic portrayals of the Magi, it had one big drawback. It did not show them as kings. As that interpretation caught on in the Middle Ages, this Ravenna mosaic played a less influential role, although it still had some effect. When the Spaniards began to explore America and met people with red skin, whom they thought to be Indians, some Spaniards concluded that Caspar had come to Bethlehem from America, a notion supported by the real possibility that Caspar's name had derived from that of an Indian king mentioned in the apocryphal *Acts of Thomas*.

So now the story of the Magi is complete? Not yet. This drama had one more act to play, and although it occurred much later than the era to which this book is devoted, it is fascinating. In 1158 an ancient chapel containing three bodies was discovered in a villa near the Italian city of Milan. The bodies were immediately believed to be those of the three kings, although no one knew how the corpses had migrated to this northern Italian city. This sounds fantastic today, but superstitious medieval people believed readily in such things.

At the time of the "discovery" of the bodies of the three kings, Milan was part of the Holy Roman Empire, which was centered in Germany. In 1164, Rainald, archbishop of the German city of Cologne and chancellor of the Holy Roman Empire, ordered the three bodies to be moved from Milan to Cologne. The bodies lie there still, encased in a huge tripartite golden coffin inside the magnificent Gothic cathedral known as the *Dreikonigsdom* or Three Kings Cathedral. A century after the transfer, however, Marco Polo, the famous Venetian explorer, challenged the identification of the bodies as those of the three kings. He reported that he had seen the three kings' tombs in Persia, but most Western European Christians rejected his claim, preferring to think that the three kings rested in a Latin Christian kingdom.

AN OBSCURE ASIAN BISHOP

The ecumenical Council of Nicea met in 325 to deal with the question of the Trinity. Tradition claimed that 318 bishops attended the council. Most are now anonymous, while some are known to us only by name. Some few are known by their reputations as theologians or as major figures in fourth-century church history. A handful of council participants became saints. Yet the best known of all the participants is a bishop from Asia Minor (modern Turkey) who at the time enjoyed no recognition outside his own diocese and who apparently played no essential role in the council. This bishop now ranks as the most famous of all Christian saints and, under a name he acquired in the nineteenth century, is literally the best known person in the world to American children. Thanks to modern communications media, he is celebrated among children virtually around the world. This obscure Asian bishop is St. Nicholas.

What we know about the historical St. Nicholas can fit into one small paragraph, so here it is: Nicholas was born in the southwestern Asia Minor town of Patara, probably in the late third century. We do not know under what circumstances he entered the clergy and became a bishop, but he occupied the see of Myra, a Mediterranean seaport. From 303 to 305 a severe persecution was inflicted on the Christians of the Eastern Mediterranean. Nicholas suffered but was not martyred in this persecution. Tradition says that he attended the Council of Nicea, and it fits the historical and geographical situations since Nicea would be a relatively simple journey from Myra. He may have been a young or old bishop at Nicea; there is no way to tell. He was buried in Myra, and his cult was initially a local one in the area around his episcopal city. Aside from that, we know nothing about Nicholas historically. His feast day is December 6, presumably the date of his death.

Legends about saints grew quickly in the early Middle Ages, and if the legends and/or the saint were striking enough, the cult would spread to the larger Church. The first written account of Nicholas dates from the eighth century, but evidence survives of an earlier cult. Because Myra was a seaport, the first trace of a Nicholas cult is for a safe voyage, something which could hardly be taken for granted in the ancient and medieval worlds. But Nicholas was not the only protector against the dangers of a voyage. There was also the pagan sea god Poseidon, and by the High Middle Ages Nicholas had picked up some of Poseidon's attributes after devotion to that god had ceased. Specifically Nicholas was pictured riding a white horse as did Poseidon; the white horse symbolized the crest of a wave.

Miraculous tales about Nicholas soon spread from the voyage to the cargo. People invoked Nicholas in times of famine because he helped grain ships to make safe voyages. A legend about him claimed that on one occasion he even paid for the grain when people could not afford it.

As people started to look for Nicholas to aid in desperate situations, his help extended in every direction. The historical Nicholas was a contemporary of the Roman emperor Constantine (306–337). A legend arose about how Nicholas intervened when the emperor was going to execute three of his officers for disloyalty. Nicholas knew that the three men were innocent, and he convinced the emperor to spare them. Similar to this was a story that he had prevented imperial soldiers from executing an innocent man in Myra; Nicholas actually grabbed the executioner's sword as it was about to come down on the man's head.

These were very dramatic tales, but the most famous of all dealt with an impending domestic tragedy. It supposedly occurred when he was a bishop. A man in Myra had three daughters, but he had no money for their dowries. (In those days it was a disgrace for a woman not to marry, and a woman without a dowry often could not get married.) The father was so desperately poor that he contemplated selling his oldest daughter into an odious form of slavery.

God sent an angel to Nicholas to inform him of the situation. One night Nicholas took a bag of gold and threw it into the window of the poor family's house. When the father saw the gold the next day, he gave it to his oldest daughter for a dowry, and she was able to marry.

But the family's poverty was not alleviated, and the father did not know what to do for his second daughter. Again Nicholas threw a bag of gold into their house at night. The second daughter thus had a dowry and could be married. The father next worried about his third daughter, but by then he was convinced that this mysterious, apparently miraculous help would return.

He let it be known that he needed funds for his third daughter's dowry, and then he waited up every night to see not only if the astonishing help would come again but also to

Icon of Saint Nicholas, the Miracle Worker, 1294. *Novgorod, Russia.*
There is no image of Saint Nicholas from the Early Church.

see who provided it. When Nicholas threw in the third bag of gold, the father rushed out of the house and caught up with the bishop. He thanked Nicholas for the help and wanted to spread the word of Nicholas' good works everywhere. But Nicholas made him swear not to reveal who had helped him until after the bishop's death.

This eighth-century story became immensely popular, and, since artists assumed that the bags were round in shape, portraits of Nicholas often show him with three golden balls, representing the three bags of gold. This story about aiding the young girls helped to make Nicholas a patron of children, the basis for the eventual Santa Claus transformation.

Nicholas' cult spread to Western Europe, and it soared in popularity there when the saint's body came to the West. The Muslims had conquered Turkey in the eleventh century, and many Christians thought it unfortunate that the saint's shrine was in "infidel" territory, even though the Muslims protected the shrine and allowed Christian pilgrims to visit it. In 1087 a group of enterprising sailors from the city of Bari in southern Italy kidnapped the saint's body from Myra and brought it home, where the locals built a great cathedral to house it. To this day the body of St. Nicholas resides there. When the thirteenth-century Italian bishop Jacob of Voragine included Nicholas in his influential collection of saints' lives, *The Golden Legend*, Nicholas' prominence in the West was assured. The medieval St. Nicholas bore little resemblance to the modern one. Both literary and visual representations portrayed him as an ascetic bishop, traveling about with his staff as a symbol of his episcopal authority.

How he became Santa (= Saint) Claus (= Ni*cholas*) is a very complicated tale and well beyond the scope of this book. Suffice it to say that the American writer Washington Irving (1783–1850) portrayed him as a patron saint of the Dutch who settled New Amsterdam (later New York) and also as a giver of gifts to children on his feast day of December 6. Irving created the St. Nicholas who left his horse and wagon on the roof so he could go down the chimney. Another American writer, Clement Clarke Moore (1779–1863), in his poem for his children, "A Visit from St. Nicholas" (1821), gave him a sleigh drawn by eight flying reindeer and changed the saint's gift-giving from his feast day to Christmas Eve.

Once separated from his feast day, Nicholas lost many of his other traditional pictorial traits, such as bishop's staff and ascetic demeanor. He initially became Moore's "right jolly old elf," but was metamorphosed anew throughout the nineteenth and twentieth centuries. He achieved his currently well-known pictorial form in a Coca-Cola advertisement from 1931. It is unlikely that the historical St. Nicholas would be able to recognize himself today.

CHAPTER FIVE

The Popular Acceptance of Christmas

By the fourth century Christmas had become a major feast in most of the ancient churches. The evidence for this comes primarily from theologians and bishops, which is no surprise for an era when most people could not read or write. But is there any evidence of the popular acceptance of Christmas? No, in the sense that we do not have collectively recorded views from the common people of that era. Yes, in the sense that we have art works, sermons, liturgies, and hymns that were intended for all the people in the Church. The visual materials, the artistic images, were the "books" of those who could not read and would have been useless if they did not draw upon what the people at least partly knew and believed.

The surviving evidence originated with bishops and theologians, but clearly if sermons or liturgies or hymns had failed to win popular approval—and anyone who has ever given a presentation or presided at a ceremony knows when something fails—no one would have bothered to record and preserve them in an age when everything written had to be painfully copied by hand. So we can assume that the surviving evidence appealed to most Christians of that day and will give us some evidence of the popular acceptance of Christmas. To be sure, scholars would like to have the evidence of popular approval that we have today, such as polling, voting, book and music sales, but we must work with the ancient world on its own terms.

Before turning to the ancient evidence, we should note that the Christmas liturgical season itself encouraged the popular acceptance of the feast. The season started four weeks before the feast and extended twelve days after it. If we include Candlemas, the season extended for forty days. Regional variations made the season even longer; for instance, the church in France started the season with the feast of St. Martin of Tours on November 11, a full six weeks before Christmas. Regardless of the frequency or seriousness of their attendance at the services, the sheer size of the liturgical season made people well aware of Christmas.

CHRISTMAS AND ART

One common way of ascertaining the ancient popular mind is art. Ancient artists often did their work with the public in mind, and scholars frequently trace certain trends in the art. For example, in the last chapter we noted that fourth-century representations of the Magi included three of them in eastern dress, pictorial representations of scholarly speculations. But can we discern specifically "Christmas" art as distinct from presentations of the Infancy Narratives? With difficulty.

Today we can easily recognize images of Christmas: Santa Claus, a Christmas tree, a snow-covered house with a wreath on the front door, and similar scenes. Furthermore, because of Christmas' prominence in our culture, even scenes of the Nativity, "the first Christmas," have largely become Christmas art. But we cannot be sure of that in the ancient world. For example, scenes of the Magi appear on sarcophagi, the large stone coffins in which prominent early Christians were entombed. Clearly the art has a funereal theme. As we have seen, Matthew's gospel links the birth and death of Jesus,

Mother and Child (fourth century). *Coemeterium Maius, Rome.*

with the Gentile Magi recognizing him as did Pilate's wife while the Jewish leaders in both instances sought his death. On the sarcophagi, images of the Magi may have reminded people that the redeemer also had to die.

On the other hand, once Christmas became a feast, the Magi appeared more and more frequently. Significantly, they did so on their own and not mixed in with many other symbolic figures on the side of a sarcophagus. The old symbolism had not completely disappeared, but the independence of the Magi separated them from the traditional funereal symbols such as the sacrifice of Isaac or of Jonah as a symbol of the Resurrection. The Magi were by then best known via the Infancy Narratives, and from the fourth century until today, those gospel accounts signify Christmas to the average Christian. So we may safely say that from the fourth century onwards, representations of the Magi can be considered Christmas art.

This same situation applies to Mary in the fourth century. She appears with increasing frequency and always with her infant son. When the ecumenical Council of Ephesus declared Mary to be Mother of God in 430, artistic representations of her sitting and holding the infant Jesus became virtually universal. Not all of these representations may have had a Christmas theme as their intent. Even as early as the apocryphal gospels, Mary's virginity played a great role in the theology and devotion of many Christians. But ultimately her virginity could not be separated from the Infancy Narratives that tell of it (it appears literally nowhere else in the Bible), and since the Infancy Narratives and Christmas had become inextricably linked, every representation of mother and infant had at least Christmas overtones if not a direct Christmas theme.

CHRISTMAS AND MUSIC

Music holds an important place in our modern Christmas, and most people know the words of the more prominent hymns and carols. Do ancient Christian songs tell us about the acceptance of Christmas? Yes and No.

First, the No. In December we can hear Christmas music anywhere, such as in our homes, in our cars, in stores and malls, at social get-togethers, and even on the street. Christmas music is not tied to any one place, and we can often listen to it privately. Did the early Christian enjoy Christmas music privately? We simply do not know. Obviously lacking the audio equipment we take for granted, they would have had limited opportunity to do so, other than singing by themselves or playing a musical instrument. Furthermore, no unquestionably secular popular music, such as "Jingle Bells," survives, nor do we have reason to think that any existed. We use the catch-all term "carols" for both secular and religious Christmas songs, but in the early Church music associated with Christmas would have been hymns. Most of these were sung at liturgies, so we cannot separate the hymns from the liturgy.

Now the Yes. Liturgies had to reach and move the populace. Then as now liturgists worked to make ceremonies effective so that they conveyed the nature of the feast and simultaneously involved the participants. Then, as now, liturgists worked to improve the liturgies, especially since, with largely illiterate congregations, they could not count on people to follow along with a hymnal, missal, or book of prayers. Thus scholars are confident that the ancient liturgies give us a view of one way that Christmas reached the whole people of God.

The musical aspects of the ancient liturgies are difficult to determine because professional musicians had not yet worked out detailed systems of notation. Furthermore, many early Christian leaders had doubts about the use of music in liturgies and especially about musical instruments that, they feared, could be distracting. But most leaders supported the use of music, and they chose to follow their Jewish forebears in employing unaccompanied singing. This type of singing became standardized in the early Middle Ages and is now universally called Gregorian chant after its traditional founder, Pope Gregory I. Given the ancient Christian loyalty to tradition, scholars believe that the later manuscripts generally preserve the ancient chants.

We will look at two great hymn writers, one from the East and one from the West.

We have met Ephraem the Syrian (d. 373) several times already. He was a deacon who strongly supported the Council of Nicea and wrote against groups that opposed it. He also shared the characteristically strong Syrian devotion to Mary, and his writings helped to spread that devotion in the Near East. Most Eastern intellectuals wrote in Greek, but he wrote in his native Syriac. Although a biblical scholar as well as polemicist, he is best known as a homilist, poet, and hymnist. The Syrian church honored him with the title "the Harp of the Holy Spirit."

Ephraem liked dramatic scenes, such as the conversation he created between Mary and the Magi alluded to in the last chapter. He also liked rhetorical flourishes, such as "Blessed the Shepherd who became a Lamb for our reconciliation" or "On this day the Lord exchanged glory for shame, as being humble." But he was at his best when he related the feast to those who would sing his hymns. Here the people praise Christ directly:

> Help us to distinguish your day from all other days!
> For great is the treasure-house of the day of your birth; let it be the one who ransoms debtors!
> Great is this day above all days, for on it came forth mercy to sinners.
> A store of medicines is this thy great day, because on it shone forth the Medicine of Life to the wounded!
> A treasure of helpful graces is this day, for on it the Light gleamed forth upon our blindness!
> This day is that forerunning Cluster (of grapes), in which the cup of salvation was concealed.
> In the winter which strips the fruit of the branches off from the barren vine, Fruit sprang up unto us;
> in the cold that bares all the trees, a shoot was green for us of the house of Jesse.
> In December when the seed is hidden in the earth, there sprouted forth from the Womb the Shoot of Life.

Even in this brief selection, we see some familiar and effective themes. The Incarnation is the taking of a material body by the Son of God in order to redeem this created world. In a burst of agricultural imagery, Ephraem related the birth of Christ to the renewal of this world, but Christ's birth does this in a miraculous way. Contrary to nature, a shoot of life springs forth in December. The shoot from the house of Jesse, the father of David, reminds us of Jesus' ancestry, while the reference to the one who ransoms debtors recalls the ancient belief that the Son of God had to win us back from the sin of Adam. Associated with this was the belief that Adam's sin had wounded human nature, which explains the reference to the Medicine of Life. Finally, *the Light that gleamed forth upon our blindness* takes us back to the opening chapter of

John's gospel, "The Light shined in the darkness," as well as to Matthew's image of the star.

Ephraem covered a lot of primary points and theological themes in a short space, but in a way that moved people intellectually and emotionally.

Most important early Christian Latin writers came from North Africa or Italy, but here we have chosen to focus on a Spanish hymnist, Aurelius Prudentius Clemens (*ca.* 348–405). Prudentius was a layman and a lawyer who worked so successfully in the civil government that he received an appointment from the imperial court. At some point he had a conversion experience and abandoned public life, turning instead to the writing of Christian poetry. He wrote on theology, Scripture, spirituality, and on the Spanish Christian martyrs.

The following verses are excerpted from his "Hymn for Christmas Day":

> Now let the sky more brightly shine, / And joyful earth keep holiday!
> The radiant sun mounts high again, / Rejoicing in his former course.

> Until the slow revolving years / In centuries at length had passed,
> And He Himself vouchsafed to come / Down to the world grown old in sin.

> The Infant's feeble cry proclaimed / The springtime of the universe;
> The world reborn then cast aside / The gloom of winter's lethargy.

> At your Nativity, O Child / All hard, unfeeling things were stirred;
> The unrelenting crags grew kind / And clothed the flinty stones with grass.

> How holy, O eternal King, / Is this your crib, revered by all
> In every age, and even by beasts / Who hover near in silent awe.

Like Ephraem, Prudentius emphasized the cosmic significance of the birth of Christ, with references to the sky, earth, and sun. He also used the strong poetic image of the Garden of Eden. In *the slowing revolving years* and *the world grown old in sin*, Prudentius reminded his readers that humanity had been in sin's power since the time of Adam, but with the coming of Christ, notice that *The unrelenting crags grew kind / And clothed the flinty stones with grass*, that is, the barren places of the world have become fruitful again, a return to the Garden of Eden. Indeed, even the beasts (the ox and the donkey) stand by *in silent awe*.

Prudentius also wrote a hymn on the Epiphany. Again he chose a cosmic theme: *This is an everlasting star / That never sinks beneath the waves*, but here used as a symbol of Christ since obviously the Star of Bethlehem was not shining in Prudentius' own day. He also had a sense of the dramatic. The coming of the Magi resulted, however inadvertently, in the massacre of the Holy Innocents. Prudentius sensed the poetic potential of this story, and so he put words into the mouth of Herod:

> Let all male children be destroyed; / Search out the bosom of each nurse,
> And even at the mother's breasts / Let blades be red with infant gore.

The hymnist went on with a graphic description of what Herod's soldiers did:

> The fiendish slayer scarce can find / On little frames sufficient space
> To hold the deadly gaping wound: / The blade is wider than the throat.

These verses bring home to us in a vivid way that the victims were infants—shocking reading but surely unforgettable.

Many other early Christians composed Christmas hymns. These included the Latin writers Ambrose of Milan (*ca.* 339–397), who is also the traditional founder of Ambrosian chant, and the Greek writer Anatolius of Constantinople (d. 458) whose Christmas hymn became part of the Vespers for Christmas in the Greek Orthodox Church. Modern Christians, such as the British composer John Rutter, continue this ancient tradition.

THE "GOLDEN TONGUE"

All clergy were expected to preach, and consequently thousands of sermons survive from the early Christian period. Modern Christians may have difficulty understanding the role of the sermon in that era. Today a twenty-minute Sunday sermon would be considered long. That is largely because in an age of commercial telecommunications, we expect messages to be brief, and few of us have the attention span for oral communication that ancient people did. But in the ancient world, oral communication was the standard, and effective public speaking was essential for success in almost any public career. Many of the most famous names of the early Church were practiced rhetoricians. They could keep congregations spellbound for an hour and sometimes beyond. The greatest preacher of the age was the Syrian John Chrysostom (*ca.* 350–407). "Chrysostom" is not part of his name but a term of honor granted to him in Byzantine tradition and is now universally used. It means "the Golden Tongue." Chroniclers record that when he had finished a sermon, members of the congregation would call out, "More, more!"

Naturally these preachers gave their greatest sermons on the most important feast days, which means that some remarkably thoughtful, imaginative, and effective Christmas and Epiphany sermons have come down to us. What follows is a very small sample.

We can start with John Chrysostom, who very ingeniously focused this sermon on Joseph, a person often overlooked at Christmas. John starts with the angel's command to Joseph to take Mary and Jesus and flee to Egypt:

> And Joseph did not take offence at this saying, nor did he say to the angel: "This is hard to understand. Did you not but recently say: 'the child shall save his people,' but now he cannot save himself, and we must take flight, and go on a long journey and dwell in a foreign land? These things are contrary to what you promised." But he said nothing of the kind, for he was a man of

faith. Nor did he make inquiry as to when they would return from Egypt, even though the angel had spoken in an indefinite manner: "Be there until I tell you." Neither was Joseph regretful at this command, but rather he was understanding and obedient, bearing these trials with cheerfulness. For the loving God mingled joy with Joseph's labors, as he does for all who are devoted to him, not permitting their tribulations or their peace to be continuous, but ordering the life of the just by commingling one with the other.

This is an effective touch. Jesus is God's Son, Mary the recipient of a miracle, but Joseph is like ordinary Christians, a good person trying to do his best in circumstances that were demanding and even confusing. The central focus of the Nativity in the early Church appropriately fell upon the Lord and his mother, but John Chrysostom does not let his congregation forget the essential contribution of Joseph to the birth of the redeemer.

This next excerpt from the Golden Tongue uses familiar themes but with remarkable eloquence:

> Bethlehem this day resembles heaven. It hears from the stars the singing of angelic voices, and in place of the sun it enfolds itself on every side with the Sun of Righteousness. And ask not how this can happen, for where God wills, the order of Nature yields. For he willed, he had the power, he descended, he redeemed; all things move in obedience to God. This day He Who Is, is born; and He Who Is becomes what he was not. For he was God and became man, yet not departing from the divinity that is his.

And now we know why John's congregations shouted, "More! More!"

AMBROSE OF MILAN

Working from the biblical image of the Church as the Body of Christ, the Italian bishop Ambrose of Milan provides an insightful interpretation of the Nativity:

> Behold the beginning of the newborn Church. Christ is born, and the shepherds begin their watch; those who will gather the

flocks of the Gentiles, before living as untended beasts, into the Fold of the Lord. . . . And well do those shepherds watch whom the Lord instructs. For the flock is the people; the night is the world; and the shepherds are the Lord's ministers. . . . See the shepherds come with haste; none comes seeking Christ in sloth. . . . Because the shepherds are people of humble stature, we should not esteem lightly the testimony of their faith. For the more humble the testimony appears to human wisdom, the more precious it is to the eyes of faith. For the Lord did not seek out the schools of learning filled with the wise, but the simple people . . . for he sought not ambition, but rather it was simplicity he looked for.

The Latin word for "shepherd" is *pastor*, and this play on words allows Ambrose to picture the shepherds as those who care for the flock of the Lord—an image he combines well with the "newborn Church," that is, the newborn body of Christ. Ambrose here used Scripture to interpret Scripture. The Apostle Paul emphasized how Jesus' message came not to the wise and powerful but to the simple and humble, and Ambrose maintained this image, which was especially important in an era when the dominant aristocrats had little but contempt for the poor and lowly.

In another sermon Ambrose made use of the Roman census, an infrequent and seemingly difficult topic for a sermon:

While the secular census is referred to, the spiritual is implied, a census to be made known, not to the king of the earth but to the king of heaven. It is a profession of faith, an enrollment of souls. . . . that you may know that this is of Christ, not of Augustus, the "whole world" is ordered to be enrolled. Who could decree the enrollment of the whole world? Not of Augustus but of the Lord was it said, "The earth is the Lord's and the fullness thereof" (Ps 24:1).

This interpretation contrasts earthly and heavenly authority as it shows that the census ordered by the emperor unknowingly began the "enrollment" of people in the following of Christ.

AUGUSTINE OF HIPPO

Although a great man himself, Ambrose is best known to posterity as the teacher of Augustine of Hippo, one of the greatest thinkers in Christian history. Augustine wrote scores of learned and influential books, and yet he also proved to be an effective and conscientious bishop who during thirty-five years in office (395–430) devoted much time and energy to the administration of his North African diocese of Hippo in the difficult days of the declining Roman Empire. His congregation expected their bishop to preach, and Augustine considered preaching to be both a prerogative and a duty. For the Latin Middle Ages, Augustine's sermons were the models of the genre. The sixth-century Gallic bishop Caesarius of Arles was the first—but not the last—bishop to advise his clergy to read sermons of Augustine to the people if they could not produce good ones of their own.

Here is an excerpt from one of the many Christmas sermons he preached:

> When the Maker of Time, the Word of the Father, was made flesh, he gave us his birthday in time; and he without whose divine bidding no day runs its course, in his Incarnation reserved one day for himself. He himself with the Father precedes all spans of time, but, on this day, issuing forth from his mother, he stepped into the tide of the years.
>
> Man's Maker was made man, that he, ruler of the stars, might nurse at his mother's breasts; the Bread might be hungry, the Fountain be thirsty, the Light sleep, the Way be tired from the journey. . . .

This eloquent little passage shows how well Augustine used imagery as well as one of his favorite devices, the paradox— bread linked with hunger, a fountain with thirst.

Augustine believed the virginal conception to be a major proof of Christ's divinity. He also believed that consecrated virginity was a higher calling than marriage, although he defended marriage against the criticisms of the Manichees, a dualist sect that despised the body and a sect to which

Augustine himself had once belonged. This excerpt shows how he links Mary's virginity with the Church:

> In Mary holy virginity gave birth to Christ. In Anna the widow-hood of advanced years recognized the Child. In Elizabeth conjugal chastity and fertility of old age were put in the service of Christ. His faithful members in all stations of life brought to their Head what they were by his grace able to bring. In the same manner, because Christ is Truth, Peace, and Justice, conceive him by your faith, give birth to him through your works, so that your heart may be doing in the law of Christ what the womb of Mary did in the flesh of Christ.
>
> Moreover, why should you not be concerned in the Virgin's childbearing, seeing that you are members of Christ? Mary gave birth to your Head; the Church gave birth to you. For the Church herself is also both mother and virgin: a mother through loving charity, a virgin through the soundness of her faith and sanctity. She gives birth to peoples, but her members belong to the One only of whom she herself is the body and the spouse. In this too she bears the image of that other virgin, the fact that she is the mother of unity among many.

Is it any wonder that medieval Latin preachers considered him their model?

Sometimes Augustine exchanged eloquence for polemic. In the ancient world astrology had many devotees, and Christianity energetically opposed it. The coming of the Magi to Bethlehem seemed to give astrology some justification. After all, had not the Magi been informed of where to go by a star? This excerpt comes one of Augustine's Epiphany sermons:

> Unlearned people hold that merely because it was written in the Gospel that when Jesus was born and the magi saw his star in the East, that Christ's birth was decreed by the stars. . . . For it happened that Christ appeared, not under the star's rule but as its Ruler; because that star did not keep to the ways of the stars in the sky but showed the men who were seeking Christ the way to the place where he had been born. . . . Nor did the star itself decree the miracles of Christ; on the contrary, Christ produced it among his own miracles.

> He himself, when born of his mother, made a new star appear
> in heaven and showed it to the earth. . . . At his birth a new
> light was revealed in the star, and at his death the sun's ancient
> light was veiled. When he was born, the inhabitants of the
> heaven became radiant with new glory. . . .
>
> Let us, then, devoutly and solemnly celebrate this day on
> which the magi of the Gentiles recognized and adored
> Christ. . . .

Augustine has managed to disparage astrology while defending
the traditional Christian belief that the physical world gave
witness to Christ's birth and later to his death.

It would probably be unfair to ask any other ancient
homilist to follow Augustine, so we will just note that many
other important writers such as Pope Leo I and Caesarius of
Arles continued the genre, often with great success.

What strikes the modern Christian about the ancient
sermons is the combination of eloquence with depth. They
routinely addressed significant theological issues, such as the
Incarnation and the Trinity, which were still topics of debate
in their day. They also instructed and delighted their audi-
ences. It would be incorrect to believe that Christians all over
the Roman Empire listened to sermons as good as the ones
we have excerpted, but meaningful sermons certainly helped
to popularize the feast of Christmas.

Some random elements also helped the cause of Christmas.
The emperor Constantine liked things big (recall that he built
a city and named it after himself), and so he saw to the con-
struction of several large churches in the fourth century. His
mother Helena made pilgrimages to the Holy Land, and on
one of those trips she discovered a cave outside Bethlehem
that she believed to be the cave of the Nativity—no matter
that the gospel said manger (Luke 2:7) and it was the apocryphal *Protoevangelium of James* that said Jesus was born in
a cave. She told her son of her wondrous discovery, and he
had a huge church built over the site, the Church of the

Nativity. Although damaged in the sixth century, it was soon rebuilt by the Byzantine emperor Justinian and still stands today.

This magnificent structure did not directly affect Christians living in far-away places like Spain or Britain, but in the fourth century increasing numbers of Westerners made pilgrimages to the Holy Land and brought back accounts of what they saw, including this impressive new church in Bethlehem and the Christmas liturgies of the Holy Land. Their accounts not only made Christmas a better-known feast, but they also changed some practices, for example, the Western churches adopted the Jerusalem custom of a midnight Mass.

RELICS

Another, often dubious, practice helped to popularize Christmas, and that was the collecting of relics. It is natural for people to want see physical objects connected with important people; this applies in both the secular and religious realms. For example, visitors to Salzburg, Austria, can go to the house where Mozart grew up and see the musical instruments the great composer played as a boy. But in the modern world, we have methods of verifying whether a particular object belonged to Mozart or Jane Austen or Abraham Lincoln.

In the ancient and medieval worlds, the only reliable way to authenticate a relic was to collect objects directly from the saint while he or she was alive or to get them immediately after the saint's death. In some cases, the saint's body *was* the relic. Because the relics were thought to have great power, such as healing or guaranteeing that saint involved would protect the locals, relics became very valuable and were often sold, used as collateral, and even, as Augustine complained, stolen. (Recall the medieval theft of the body of St. Nicholas.)

But far more problematic was the potential for abuse with unauthenticated relics. Pious gullibility often prevailed. Inevitably, this applied to "relics" of the Nativity. The fifth-century Church of St. Mary Major in Rome managed to

acquire some of the wood supposedly from Jesus' manger.
The wood was placed in a silver reliquary that is still on
display in that church. The flood gates soon opened, and in
the early Middle Ages, churches claimed to have the tunic
Mary wore when she gave birth, the blanket in which the
infant Jesus was wrapped, and straw from the crib, all of these
being rather questionable items. There can be no doubt,
however, that Nativity "relics" helped to popularize Christmas
among an uneducated and credulous populace.

One of the oddest, indeed most ironic, elements in the
popular acceptance of Christmas was the feast of Saturnalia,
which lasted from December 17 to 23. To a lesser extent,
the Christians were also influenced by the Roman New Year's
feast on January 1. Both were major feasts of the pagans,
and they involved much feasting and drinking, mumming,
gambling, dancing, overturning of social roles, and gift-giving
as well as "mingling of all classes in a common jollity," as
the historian Clement Miles put it. On New Year's day the
Romans decorated their homes with lights and greenery.
Not surprisingly, the Roman populace liked those feast days
and did not wish to give them up.

Miles summed it up succinctly: "The pagan Romans became
Christian—but Saturnalia remained." Gregory of Nazianzus,
a fourth-century bishop of Constantinople, warned his congregation about feasting to excess and about wild dancing,
and he urged them to approach Christmas after a heavenly
and not an earthly manner. Other bishops shared his concern.
The sixth-century bishop Caesarius of Arles recommended
fasting on New Year's Day, the polar opposite of the traditional way of celebrating the feast.

Yet this Saturnalian influence was not totally negative. Not
all feasting must lead to gluttony; not all dancing must lead
to frenzy; and as for gambling, what would many churches do
without bingo and "Las Vegas Night"? To be sure, the tempta-
tion to overdo the celebrating would always be there, as it is
today, but, unlike the Puritans, most Christians see nothing

wrong with having fun. As any modern Christian knows, the secular elements provide many of the joys of the season—decorating a tree, seeing the lights in houses and in store windows, purchasing gifts for loved ones, attending choral concerts, getting together with friends and co-workers—and yet Christians can still reverently attend Advent and Christmas services. The ancient Roman Christians shared that view. As Miles puts it, "Who can wonder that Christmas contains incongruous elements, for old things, loved by the people, cannot easily be uprooted."

Clearly the Christians could not celebrate Saturnalia, which was, after all, named for a pagan god, nor could they keep New Year's as the pagans did, but they could bring elements of those celebrations into their Christmas festivities. The non-religious festive element probably went a long way toward making the religious festival a popular one.

These early celebrations kept growing throughout the Middle Ages and have continued until today. In fact, this phenomenon disproves a very common misconception about Christmas, that it was a quiet religious holiday with no secular overtones until nineteenth-century capitalists turned it into a secular holiday in order to make money. Christmas has always had a secular element, which, if applied sensibly, can flourish alongside the religious element and even add to the season.

Epilogue

This brief book has taken Christmas into the sixth century, that is, to the end of the Ancient World and the beginning of the Middle Ages. Christmas came a long way in those six centuries, from not even existing to possibly starting as a Gnostic feast to oppose Egyptian paganism to being a counter to the feast of the Unconquered Sun to becoming involved in Christology and Mariology to creating the legends of the Magi to becoming a regular part of Christian life. It is a remarkable story, and one that is a delight to research and tell.

But the story of Christmas goes on so much longer, well beyond the compass of this volume, although it is a good topic for another book or two.

Possibly the most important change for Christmas lay just over our chronological horizon. When early medieval missionaries brought the faith to the northern European pagan barbarians, that is, the Germans and the Celts, they brought Christmas to peoples who lived in serious winter environments and who had long-established winter customs and festivals. In the northern environment Christmas became the winter feast it could never have become in Egypt or North Africa. This trait has stayed with Christmas ever since; today even in warm areas Christmas decorations and cards show a snow-covered roof or people bundled up for a sleigh ride.

Christmas flourished in the Middle Ages but often had rough overtones, such as excessive eating, drinking, and gambling, all leftovers from Saturnalia. The feast suffered a decline after the Reformation. Some rigorous Christians had doubts about whether it should be observed since it is not in the Bible (recall our early distinction that the Bible tells of the Nativity but not of Christmas, the feast honoring the Nativity), but most other Christians worked to tone down the more raucous elements of the celebration rather than to abandon it. In the seventeenth century in both England and New England, Puritans rejected Christmas as unbiblical and loathed it for its "papist" name, that is, "Christ's Mass," and they actually outlawed Christmas where and when they dominated the government. But in both England and America the views of larger bodies of Christians prevailed, and in the eighteenth century Christmas continued to be observed, although primarily as an adult holiday, replete with much food and alcohol.

The nineteenth century brought about three great changes: the invention Santa Claus, the transformation of Christmas into a children's holiday, and the introduction of massive commercialization, traits which have remained largely unchanged. Indeed, the main contribution of the twentieth and twenty-first centuries has been to expand the range of Christmas via the technological and communications revolutions— why go to the department store if your little computer whiz can contact Santa on the Net?

And, of course, believing Christians still celebrate Christmas as the birthday of their Lord, just as they did all those centuries ago.

Christmas will always change, but it will never disappear. For that, we can thank the ancient Christians who made this remarkable feast such an essential part of their lives.

The Gospel Infancy Narratives

THE GOSPEL ACCORDING TO MATTHEW

The Genealogy of Jesus

1,1. An account of the genealogy of Jesus the Messiah, the son of David, the son of Abraham.

(2) Abraham was the father of Isaac, and Isaac the father of Jacob, and Jacob the father of Judah and his brothers, (3) and Judah the father of Perez and Zerah by Tamar, and Perez the father of Hezron, and Hezron the father of Aram, (4) and Aram the father of Aminadab, and Aminadab the father of Nahshon, and Nahshon the father of Salmon, (5) and Salmon the father of Boaz by Rahab, and Boaz the father of Obed by Ruth, and Obed the father of Jesse, (6) and Jesse the father of King David.

And David was the father of Solomon by the wife of Uriah, (7) and Solomon the father of Rehoboam, and Rehoboam the father of Abijah, and Abijah the father of Asaph, (8) and Asaph the father of Jehoshaphat, and Jehoshaphat the father of Joram, and Joram the father of Uzziah, (9) and Uzziah the father of Jotham, and Jotham the father of Ahaz, and Ahaz the father of Hezekiah, (10) and Hezekiah the father of

Manasseh, and Manasseh the father of Amos, and Amos the
father of Josiah, (11) and Josiah the father of Jechoniah and
his brothers at the time of deportation to Babylon.

(12) And after the deportation to Babylon: Jechoniah was
the father of Salathiel, and Salathiel the father of Zerubbabel,
(13) and Zerubbabel the father of Abiud, and Abiud the father
of Eliakim, and Eliakim the father of Azor, (14) and Azor the
father of Zadok, and Zadok the father of Achim, and Achim
the father of Eliud, (15) and Eliud the father of Eleazar, and
Eleazar the father of Matthan, and Matthan the father of
Jacob, (16) and Jacob the father of Joseph the husband of
Mary, of whom Jesus was born, who is called the Messiah.

(17) So all the generations from Abraham to David are
fourteen generations, and from David to the deportation to
Babylon, fourteen generations; and from the deportation
to Babylon to the Messiah, fourteen generations.

The Birth of Jesus

(18) Now the birth of Jesus the Messiah took place in this
way. When his mother Mary had been engaged to Joseph,
but before they lived together, she was found to be with child
from the Holy Spirit. (19) Her husband Joseph, being a
righteous man and unwilling to expose her to public disgrace,
planned to dismiss her quietly. (20) But just when he had
resolved to do so, an angel of the Lord appeared to him in a
dream and said, "Joseph, son of David, do not be afraid to
take Mary as your wife, for the child conceived in her is from
the Holy Spirit. (21) She will bear a son, and you are to name
him Jesus, for he will save his people from their sins."
(22) All this took place to fulfill what had been spoken by the
Lord through the prophet: (23) *"Look, the virgin shall conceive and bear a son, and they shall name him Emmanuel,"*
which means "God is with us." (24) When Joseph awoke from
sleep, he did as the angel of the Lord commanded him; he
took her as his wife, (25) but had no marital relations with
her until she had born a son; (26) and he named him Jesus.

The Visit of the Magi

2, 1. In the time of King Herod, after Jesus was born in Bethlehem of Judea, wise men came to Jerusalem, (2) asking "Where is the child who has been born king of the Jews? For we observed his star in the east and have come to pay him homage." (3) When King Herod heard this, he was frightened, and all Jerusalem with him; (4) and calling together all the chief priests and scribes of the people, he inquired of them where the Messiah was to be born. (5) They told him, "In Bethlehem of Judea; for so it has been written by the prophet: (6) *"And you, Bethlehem, in the land of Judah, are by no means least among the rulers of Judah; for from you shall come a ruler who is to shepherd my people Israel."*

(7) Then Herod secretly called for the wise men and learned from them the exact time the star had appeared. (8) Then he sent them to Bethlehem, saying, "Go and search diligently for the child; and when you have found him, bring me word so that I may also go and pay him homage." (9) When they had heard the king, they set out; and there, ahead of them, went the star that they had seen at its rising, until it stopped at the place where the child was. (10) When they saw that the star had stopped, they were overwhelmed with great joy. (11) On entering the house, they saw the child with Mary his mother; and they knelt down and paid him homage. Then, opening their treasure chests, they offered him gifts of gold, frankincense, and myrrh. (12) And having been warned in a dream not to return to Herod, they left for their own country by another road.

The Escape to Egypt

(13) Now after they had left, an angel of the Lord appeared to Joseph in a dream and said, "Get up, take the child and his mother, and flee to Egypt, and remain there until I tell you; for Herod is about to search for the child, to destroy him." (14) Then Joseph got up, took the child and his mother by night, and went to Egypt, (15) and remained there until the

death of Herod. This was to fulfill what had been spoken by the Lord through the prophet, *"Out of Egypt I have called my son."*

The Massacre of the Innocents

(16) When Herod saw that he had been tricked by the wise men, he was infuriated, and he sent and killed all the male children in and around Bethlehem who were two years old or under, according to the time that he had learned from the wise men. (17) Then was fulfilled what had been spoken through the prophet Jeremiah, (18) *"A voice was heard in Ramah, wailing and loud lamentations, Rachel weeping for her children; she refused to be consoled, because they are no more."*

The Return from Egypt

(19) When Herod died, an angel of the Lord suddenly appeared in a dream to Joseph in Egypt and said, (20) "Get up, take the child and his mother, and go to the land of Israel, for those who were seeking the child's life are dead." (21) Then Joseph got up, took the child and his mother, and went to the land of Israel. (22) But when he heard that Archelaus was ruling over Jerusalem in place of his father Herod, he was afraid to go there. And after being warned in a dream, he went away to the district of Galilee. (23) There he made his home in a town called Nazareth, so that what had been spoken through the prophets might be fulfilled, *"He will be called a Nazorean."*

THE GOSPEL ACCORDING TO LUKE
Dedication to Theophilus

1.1. Since many have undertaken to set down an orderly account of the events that have been fulfilled among us, (2) just as they were handed on to us by those who from the beginning were eyewitnesses and servants of the word, (3) I too decided, after investigating everything carefully from the very first, to write an orderly account for you, most

excellent Theophilus, (4) so that you may know the truth
concerning the things about which you have been instructed.

The Announcement of the Birth of John the Baptist

(5) In the days of King Herod of Judea, there was a priest
named Zechariah, who belonged to the priestly order of
Abijah. His wife was a descendant of Aaron, and her name
was Elizabeth. (6) Both of them were righteous before God,
living blamelessly according to all the commandments and
regulations of the Lord. (7) But they had no children because
Elizabeth was barren, and both were getting on in years.

(8) Once when he was serving before God and his section
was on duty, (9) he was chosen by lot, according to the
custom of the priesthood, to enter the sanctuary of the Lord
and offer incense. (10) Now at the time of the incense offer-
ing, the whole assembly of the people was praying outside.
(11) Then there appeared to him an angel of the Lord, stand-
ing at the right side of the altar of incense. (12) When
Zechariah saw him, he was terrified; and fear overwhelmed
him. (13) But the angel said to him, "Do not be afraid,
Zechariah, for your prayer has been heard. Your wife Elizabeth
will bear you a son, and you will name him John. (14) You
will have great joy and gladness, and many will rejoice at his
birth, (15) for he will be great in the sight of the Lord. He
must never drink wine or strong drink; even before his birth
he will be filled with the Holy Spirit. (16) He will turn many
of the people of Israel to the Lord their God. (17) With the
spirit and power of Elijah he will go before him, to turn the
hearts of parents to their children, and the disobedient to the
wisdom of the righteous; to make ready a people prepared for
the Lord." (18) Zechariah said to the angel, "How will I know
that this is so? For I am an old man, and my wife is getting
on in years." (19) The angel replied, "I am Gabriel. I stand in
the presence of God, and I have been sent to speak to you and
to bring you this good news. (20) But now, because you did
not believe my words, which will be fulfilled in their time,

you will become mute, unable to speak until the day these things occur."

(21) Meanwhile the people were waiting for Zechariah and wondered at his delay in the sanctuary. (22) When he did come out, he could not speak to them, and they realized that he had seen a vision in the sanctuary. He kept motioning to them and remained unable to speak. (23) When his time of service was ended, he went to his home.

(24) After those days, his wife Elizabeth conceived, and for five months she remained in seclusion. She said, (25) "This is what the Lord has done for me when he looked favorably on me and took away the disgrace I have endured among my people."

The Announcement of the Birth of Jesus

(26) In the sixth month the angel Gabriel was sent by God to a town in Galilee called Nazareth, (27) to a virgin engaged to a man whose name was Joseph, of the house of David. The virgin's name was Mary. (28) And he came to her and said, "Greetings, favored one! The Lord is with you." (29) But she was much perplexed by his words and pondered what sort of greeting this might be. (30) The angel said to her, "Do not be afraid, Mary, for you have found favor with God. (31) And now, you will conceive in your womb and bear a son, and you will name him Jesus. (32) He will be great, and will be called the Son of the Most High, and the Lord God will give to him the throne of his ancestor David. (33) He will reign over the house of Jacob forever, and of his kingdom there will be no end." (34) Mary said to the angel, "How can this be, since I am a virgin?" (35) The angel said to her, "The Holy Spirit will come upon you, and the power of the Most High will over-shadow you; therefore the child to be born will be holy; he will be called the Son of God. (36) And now, your relative Elizabeth in her old age has also conceived a son; and this is the sixth month for her who was said to be barren. (37) For nothing will be impossible with God." (38) Then Mary said,

"Here am I, the servant of the Lord; let it be with me according to your word." Then the angel departed from her.

Mary Visits Elizabeth

(39) In those days Mary set out and went with haste to a Judean town in the hill country, (40) where she entered the house of Zechariah and greeted Elizabeth. (41) When Elizabeth heard Mary's greeting, the child leapt in her womb. And Elizabeth was filled with the Holy Spirit (42) and exclaimed with a loud cry, "Blessed are you among women, and blessed is the fruit of your womb. (43) And why has this happened to me, that the mother of my Lord comes to me? (44) For as soon as I heard the sound of your greeting, the child in my womb leapt for joy. (45) And blessed is she who believed that there would be a fulfillment of what was spoken to her by the Lord."

The Magnificat

(46) And Mary cried, "My soul magnifies the Lord,
(47) and my spirit rejoices in God my savior,
(48) for he has looked with favor on the lowliness of his
     servant.
          Surely, from now on all generations will call me blessed;
(49) for the Mighty One has done great things for me, and
     holy is his name.
(50) His mercy is for those who fear him from generation to
     generation.
(51) He has shown strength with his arm;
          he has scattered the proud in the thoughts of their
          hearts.
(52) He has brought down the powerful from their thrones,
     and lifted up the lowly;
(53) he has filled the hungry with good things, and sent the
     rich away empty.
(54) He has helped his servant Israel, in remembrance of his
     mercy,

(55) according to the promise he made to our ancestors,
      to Abraham and to his descendants forever."
(56) And Mary remained with her about three months and
  then returned to her home.

The Birth of John the Baptist

(57) Now the time came for Elizabeth to give birth, and she
bore a son. (58) Her neighbors and relatives heard that the
Lord had shown great mercy to her, and they rejoiced
with her.

(59) On the eighth day they came to circumcise the child,
and they were going to name him Zechariah after his father.
(60) But his mother said, "No, he is to be called John."
(61) They said to her, "None of your relatives has this name."
(62) Then they began motioning to his father to find out what
name he wanted to give him. (63) He asked for a writing
tablet and wrote, "His name is John." And all of them were
amazed. (64) Immediately his mouth was opened and his
tongue freed, and he began to speak, praising God. (65) Fear
came over all their neighbors, and all these things were talked
about throughout the entire hill country of Judea. (66) All
who heard them pondered them and said, "What then will
this child become?" For, indeed, the hand of the Lord was
with him.

The Benedictus

(67) Then his father Zechariah was filled with the Holy
Spirit and spoke this prophecy:
(68) "Blessed be the Lord of Israel,
      for he has looked favorably upon his people and
        redeemed them.
(69) He has raised up a mighty savior for us
      in the house of his servant David,
(70) as he spoke through the mouth of his holy prophets from
      of old,

(71)   that we would be saved from our enemies and from
                 the hand of all who hate us.
(72) Thus he has shown the mercy promised to our ancestors,
                 and has remembered his holy covenant,
(73) the oath that he swore to our ancestor Abraham,
                 to grant us (74) that we, being rescued from the
                 hands of our enemies,
           might serve him without fear, (75) in holiness and right-
                 eousness
           before him all our days.
(76) And you, child, will be called the prophet of the Most High;
                 for you will go before the Lord to prepare his ways,
(77) to give knowledge of salvation to his people
                 by the forgiveness of their sins.
(78) By the tender mercy of our God,
                 the dawn from on high will break upon us,
(79) to give light to those who sit in darkness and in the
                 shadow of death,
                 to guide our feet on the way to peace."
   (80) The child grew and became strong in spirit, and he was
in the wilderness until the day of his appearance publicly to
Israel.

The Birth of Jesus

   2,1. In those days a decree went forth from Caesar Augustus
that a census of the whole world should be taken. (2) This
was the first census and was taken while Quirinius was
governor of Syria. (3) All went to their own towns to be
registered. (4) Joseph went from the town of Nazareth in
Galilee to Judea, to the city of David which is called
Bethlehem, because he was descended from the house and
family of David. (5) He went to be registered with Mary, to
whom he was engaged and who was expecting a child.
(6) While they were there, the time came for her to deliver her
first child. (7) And she gave birth to her firstborn son and

wrapped him in bands of cloth, and laid him in a manger, because there was no room for them in the inn.

The Shepherds and the Angels

(8) And in that region there were shepherds living in the fields, keeping watch over their flock by night. (9) Then an angel of the Lord stood before them, and the glory of the Lord shone around them, and they were terrified. (10) But the angel said to them, "Do not be afraid; for see—I am bringing you good news of great joy for all the people: (11) to you is born this day in the city of David a Savior, who is the Messiah, the Lord. (12) This will be a sign for you: you will find the child wrapped in bands of cloth and lying in a manger." (13) And suddenly there was with the angel a multitude of the heavenly host, praising God and saying,
(14) "Glory to God in the highest heaven, and on earth peace among those whom he favors." *(In Latin: "Gloria in excelsis Deo, et in terra pax hominibus bonae voluntatis," thus the familiar if inaccurate, "Glory to God in the highest, and on earth peace to men of good will.")*

(15) When the angels had left them and gone into heaven, the shepherds said to one another, "Let us go now to Bethlehem and see this thing that has taken place, which the Lord made known to us." (16) So they went with haste and found Mary and Joseph, and the child lying in the manger. (17) When they saw this, they made known what had been told them about this child; (18) and all who heard them were amazed at what the shepherds told them. (19) But Mary treasured all these words and pondered them in her heart. (20) The shepherds returned, glorifying and praising God for all they had heard and seen, as it had been told them.

Jesus Is Named and Presented in the Temple

(21) After eight days had passed, it was time to circumcise the child; and he was called Jesus, the name given by the angel before he was conceived in the womb.

(22) When the time came for the purification according to the Law of Moses, they brought him up to Jerusalem to present him to the Lord (23) [as it is written in the law of the Lord, "Every firstborn male shall be designated as holy to the Lord"], (24) and they offered a sacrifice according to what is stated in the law of the Lord, "a pair of turtledoves or two young pigeons."

(25) Now there was a man in Jerusalem whose name was Simeon; this man was righteous and devout, looking forward to the consolation of Israel, and the Holy Spirit rested on him. (26) It had been revealed to him by the Holy Spirit that he would not see death before he had seen the Lord's Messiah. (27) Guided by the Spirit, Simeon came into the temple; and when the parents brought in the child Jesus, to do for him what was customary under the law,

The Nunc Dimittis

(28) Simeon took him in his arms and praised God, saying,
(29) "Master, you are now dismissing your servant in peace,
     according to your word;
(30) for my eyes have seen your salvation,
(31)   which you prepared in the presence of all peoples,
(32) a light for revelation to the Gentiles
     and for glory to your people Israel."

(33) And the child's father and mother were amazed at what was being said about him. (34) Then Simeon blessed them and said to his mother Mary, "This child is destined for the falling and the rising of many in Israel, and to be a sign that will be opposed (35) so that the inner thoughts of many will be revealed—and a sword will pierce your own soul too."

(36) There was also a prophet, Anna the daughter of Phanuel, of the tribe of Asher. She was of a great age, having lived with her husband seven years after her marriage, (37) then as a widow to the age of eighty-four. She never left the temple but worshiped there with fasting and prayer night and day. (38) At that moment she came, and began to praise

God and to speak about the child to all who were looking for the redemption of Jerusalem.

(39) When they had finished everything required by the law of the Lord, they returned to Galilee, to their own town of Nazareth. (40) The child grew and became strong, filled with wisdom; and the favor of God was upon him.

The Boy Jesus in the Temple

(41) Now every year his parents went to Jerusalem for the festival of the Passover. (42) And when he was twelve years old, they went up as usual for the festival. (43) When the festival was ended and they started to return, the boy Jesus stayed behind in Jerusalem, but his parents did not know it. (44) Assuming that he was in the group of travelers, they went a day's journey. Then they started to look for him among their relatives and friends. (45) When they did not find him, they returned to Jerusalem to search for him. (46) After three days they found him in the temple, sitting among the teachers, listening to them and asking them questions. (47) And all who heard him were amazed at his understanding and his answers. (48) When his parents saw him, they were astonished; and his mother said to him, "Child, why have you treated us like this? Look, your father and I have been searching for you in great anxiety." (49) He said to them, "Why were you searching for me? Did you not know that I must be in my Father's house?" (50) But they did not understand what he said to them. (51) Then he went down with them and came to Nazareth, and was obedient to them. His mother treasured all these things in her heart.

(52) And Jesus increased in wisdom and in years, and in divine and human favor.

Further Reading

ANCIENT WRITERS

Collections of Texts

Elliott, J. K., ed. *The Apocryphal Jesus*. New York, 1996.

Schneemelcher, Wilhelm, ed. *New Testament Apocrypha, Volume One: Gospels and Related Writings*, rev. ed. R. McL. Wilson, trans. Louisville, 1991.

Toal, M. F., ed. *Patristic Homilies on the Gospels, I: From the First Sunday of Advent to Quinquagesima*. Chicago, 1955.

Works of individual authors can be found in these series:
ACW – Ancient Christian Writers (1946–) Westminster, Md., Mahwah, N.J.
ANF – Ante-Nicene Fathers (1885, repr. 1994) Peabody, Mass.
FC – Fathers of the Church (1946–) Washington, D.C.
NPNF – Nicene and Post-Nicene Fathers (1887, repr. 1994) Peabody, Mass.

MODERN WRITERS

Bowler, Gerry. *The World Encyclopedia of Christmas*. Toronto, 2000.

Bradshaw, Paul. *The Search for the Origins of Christian Worship*. New York, 2002.

Brown, Raymond. *The Birth of the Messiah*, 2nd ed. New York, 1993.

_____, *et al. Mary in the New Testament.* Philadelphia, 1978.

Connell, Martin. "The Origins and Evolution of Advent in the West." In *Between Memory and Hope*, Maxwell Johnson, ed. Collegeville, Minn., 2000, 349–71.

Dearmer, Percy, ed. *The Oxford Book of Carols.* London, 1999.

Dohmen, Christoph. *No Trace of Christmas? Discovering Advent in the Old Testament.* Collegeville, Minn., 2000.

Foley, Edward. *Foundations of Christmas Music.* Collegeville, Minn., 1996.

Granfield, Patrick, and Jungmann, Josef, ed. *Kyriakon*, 2 vols. Münster, 1970.

Jensen, Robin. *Understanding Early Christian Art.* London, 2000.

Johnson, Maxwell, ed. *From Memory to Hope.* Collegeville, Minn., 2000.

Kelly, Joseph. *The World of the Early Christians.* Collegeville, Minn., 1997.

Kidger, Mark. *The Star of Bethlehem: An Astronomer's View.* Princeton, 1999.

Metzger, Bruce. "Naming the Nameless in the New Testament." In *Kyriakon, Volume I*, Patrick Granfield and Josef Jungmann, eds., 79–99.

Miles, Clement. *Christmas Customs and Traditions.* New York, 1912, repr. 1976.

Molnar, Michael. *The Star of Bethlehem: The Legacy of the Magi.* New Brunswick, N.J., 2000.

O'Connell, Charles. "Court Martial." In *An Oxford Book of Christmas Stories*, Dennis Pepper, ed., 221–23.

Pepper, Dennis, ed. *An Oxford Book of Christmas Stories.* Oxford, 1988.

Restad, Penne. *Christmas in America.* New York, 1995.

Roll, Susan. *Toward the Origins of Christmas.* Kampen, The Netherlands, 1995.

Talley, Thomas. *The Origins of the Liturgical Year.* Collegeville, Minn., 1991.

Trexler, Richard. *The Journey of the Magi*. Princeton, 1997.

Wilson, Jacqueline. "Call Me Blessed." In *An Oxford Book of Christmas Stories*, Dennis Pepper, ed., 125–29.

REFERENCES

On Joseph as Jesus' father according to Jewish law, see Brown, 135.

Kidger on DO Aquilae, 275.

The *Protoevangelium of James*, the *Arabic Infancy Gospel*, and the *Gospel of Pseudo-Matthew* can be found in Schneemelcher, vol. 1.

The *Infancy Gospel of Thomas*, the *Latin Infancy Gospel in the Arundel Manuscript*, and the *Acts of Pilate* can be found in Eliott.

"Cherry Tree Carol" in *Oxford Book of Carols*, 143.

O'Connnor's and Wilson's stories can be found in *An Oxford Book of Christmas Stories*.

Quotations from Leo the Great's Christmas sermons in Roll, 154.

Quotations from Clement of Alexandria from his book *Stromateis*, bk.1, in ANF 2.

For the impact of ending the feast of the Circumcision on Jewish-Christian relations, see Dohmen, 90.

On "The Twelve Days of Christmas," see Bowler, 231.

Citations from ancient writers about the Magi found in ANF under their names with references to the Magi in the indexes.

Metzger's remarks about the Magi are from p. 80 of his essay.

Citations from Ephraem on pp. 227–30 of NPNF 13.

Citation from Prudentius on pp. 78–92 of FC 43.

Citations from John Chrysostom on pp. 129 and 250 of Toal.

Citations from Ambrose on pp. 120, 136–37 of Toal.

Citations from Augustine on pp. 107, 114, and 157–58 of ACW 15.

Citations from Miles' book on pp. 25 and 166; Miles also quoted on p. 5 of Restad.